Starting
Your Day
Right

Starting Your Day Right

DEVOTIONS FOR EACH MORNING OF THE YEAR

Joyce Meyer

WARNER
Faith™

A Division of AOL Time Warner Book Group

Warner Books, Inc., 1271 Avenue of the Americas,
New York, NY 10020
Visit our Web site at www.twbookmark.com
A Division of AOL Time Warner Book Group
The Warner Faith name and logo are registered trademarks
of Warner Books, Inc.
Book design by Fearn Cutler de Vicq
Printed in the USA
ISBN 0-446-53265-7

My soul, wait only upon God *and* silently submit to Him; for my hope *and* expectation are from Him.

PSALM 62:5

Introduction

God wants you to enjoy your life. Jesus said, "I came that they may have *and* enjoy life, and have it in abundance (to the full, till it overflows)" (John 10:10). Your days can be filled with an overflowing joy that will spill into the lives of others. You can experience this joy all day if you learn to start your day right—by spending time with God, reading His Word, praying, and listening for His direction.

Listening to God each morning fills you with expectancy and favor for a better day, and those days add up to a better life. The Lord wants you to have Him clearly in sight in order to follow Him. He is willing to wake you in the morning and make your ear alert to His instruction. If you will seek Him with all your heart, He will renew your strength and make clear your path (see Isaiah 40:31; Proverbs 3:6).

I have written this book to remind you of the benefits of starting your day with God. It is not written to replace your personal time with Him, but simply to enhance it and to point you to your own daily encounter with Him so that you will enjoy every day of your life. He will teach you to balance out your extremes, gain self-control, and live in a way that has a positive impact on others. I encourage you to seek God early each morning and to wait on Him to write in your spirit direction for the day. God will fill your heart with knowledge that will enlighten you at the right time. Once you experience the empowerment of beginning your day with God, you will never want to start your day without Him.

Starting
Your Day
Right

Start Your Day Right

When I said, My foot is slipping, Your mercy and loving-kindness, O Lord, held me up.

PSALM 94:18

Some people seem to start their day on the "wrong foot." They feel all right when they wake up, but as soon as something goes wrong, they lose their footing and walk with a "loser's limp" the rest of the day. Once they are off to a bad start, it seems they never catch up.

If someone offends us early in the morning, our anger can keep us defensive all day. If we start the day rushing, it seems we never slow down. But today our feet can be firmly planted in God's Word. There will be no "bad day" when God's Word supports, strengthens, and directs us.

Get Up and Get Going

I am weary with my groaning; all night I soak my pillow with tears, I drench my couch with my weeping . . . Depart from me, all you workers of iniquity, for the Lord has heard the voice of my weeping *(emphasis mine).*

PSALM 6:6, 8

Even before we are totally awake, Satan is bidding to deceive us and is ready to plant defeating thoughts in our mind. He wants us to be hopeless, faithless, and negative. He definitely doesn't want us to *be* positive when we get up. He wants us to have a bad attitude and be selfish and self-centered, full of hatred, bitterness, resentment, doubt, unbelief, and fear — to be mad at everybody.

But thank God, through Jesus Christ, we have been redeemed from all of those negative patterns. We can resist the devil and trust God's power in order to live victoriously today.

Keep in Touch with God

*Blessed (happy, fortunate, prosperous, and
enviable) is the man who walks and lives not in the
counsel of the ungodly [following their advice,
their plans and purposes] . . . But his delight and
desire are in the law of the Lord, and on His law
(the precepts, the instructions, the teachings
of God) he habitually meditates (ponders
and studies) by day and by night.*

PSALM 1:1—2

Keep in touch with God today; stay tuned
to His voice. You may have a plan for the
day, but God may lead you in a totally different direction if you are sensitive to the Holy Ghost. Be
brave enough to flow with what you feel in your
heart God wants you to do.

Today is going to be a good day. Listen for the
voice of God to lead you. Be determined to walk in
the Spirit and stay in the flow of God's leading today.

Avoid the Slingers

O God, You are my God, earnestly will I seek You;
my inner self thirsts for You . . . in a dry and weary
land where no water is . . . I have looked upon You
in the sanctuary to see Your power and Your glory.
Because Your loving-kindness is better than life,
my lips shall praise You.

PSALM 63:1—3

There were people in the Bible called slingers who defeated their enemies by slinging stones and throwing dirt into their wells, contaminating their life source of water (see 2 Kings 3:25). We all know people who sling accusation, judgment, criticism, and faultfinding at others. We certainly don't want slingers in our life, and we don't want to become slingers either.

Don't be a slinger who contaminates your own faith or the faith of those around you. Spending time with God will fill you with "living water" (see John 7:38). You will be edified and become a source of encouragement for others all day long.

Get in the Flow

You cause them to drink of the stream of Your pleasures. For with You is the fountain of life; in Your light do we see light. O continue Your loving-kindness to those who know You, Your righteousness (salvation) to the upright in heart.

PSALM 36:8—10

I have never been much of a swimmer. I may not be the best at fighting the current, but I can float. It is wonderful just to trust the water to keep us up and go with the flow. We can trust God to keep us afloat through the rapids and lead us to still waters.

The Bible says God's mercy and loving-kindness are "new *every* morning" (see Lamentations 3:22—23). His mercy isn't just there waiting for us; it is *new*, fresh, flowing, and powerful every new day. We need to get in the flow of God's river of life early each day and learn to float on the power of His presence.

Get Rest

As for me, I will continue beholding Your face in righteousness (rightness, justice, and right standing with You); I shall be fully satisfied, when I awake [to find myself] beholding Your form [and having sweet communion with You].

PSALM 17:15

Each evening the sun sets on all of our problems and on all of the mistakes we made that day. But something marvelous happens to us as we sleep — the Lord gives us rest physically, mentally, and emotionally. We are renewed and rejuvenated to face the next day.

Today we may wake up with the same problems we had when we went to bed, problems that yesterday we felt we just couldn't take anymore. But somehow today, after proper rest and sleep, we think, *I can do it; I can face it again.* God promises to renew our strength when we rest in Him.

Rejoice Today

Let the hearts of those rejoice who seek the Lord!
Seek the Lord and His strength; yearn for and seek
His face and to be in His presence continually!
[Earnestly] remember the marvelous deeds which He
has done, His miracles, and the judgments He uttered.

1 CHRONICLES 16:10–12

Many people don't realize how important the morning is, especially those first moments of time that we are awake. God calls the sun to rise for us. He is eager for us to wake up and talk to Him again.

David the psalmist talked a lot about mornings, saying "This is the day that the Lord has made; I *will* rejoice and be glad in it" (see Psalm 118:24). David didn't always *feel* like rejoicing, but he *decided* to rejoice in God's new day.

As soon as you get up, look at yourself in the mirror, smile, and say, "I am going to have a good day because Jesus loves me."

Start Out Joyfully

You try the heart and delight in uprightness. In the uprightness of my heart I have freely offered all these things. And now I have seen with joy Your people who are present here offer voluntarily and freely to You. O Lord . . . keep forever such purposes and thoughts in the minds of Your people, and direct and establish their hearts toward You.

I CHRONICLES 29:17—18

My husband always seems happy. Within five minutes of waking, Dave is humming, singing, or listening to music as he gets ready for the day. Years ago I didn't want music on in the morning. I didn't want singing or humming or noise of any kind. I wanted silence so I could think.

Today I still need a little more quiet than Dave does in the morning. But we have both found the way to start our day out right. We set our hearts and minds to follow God. And it works.

Listen for His Purpose

Who is the man who reverently fears and worships the Lord? Him shall He teach in the way that he should choose. He himself shall dwell at ease . . . The secret [of the sweet, satisfying companionship] of the Lord have they who fear (revere and worship) Him.

PSALM 25:12—14

It is God who wakes us each morning. If He didn't keep us alive overnight, it wouldn't matter what kind of an alarm clock we had! The prophet said, "God wakens me morning by morning, and He wakens me for a purpose so that I can hear; I am like a disciple who is taught" (see Isaiah 50:4).

Before you even get out bed, listen to hear what God has to say to you. It will be a good day if you start it with a ready ear, taking time to listen to Him. God is eager to reveal today's plan to you.

Expect Something New

In the morning, O LORD, you hear my voice;
in the morning I lay my requests before you
and wait in expectation.

PSALM 5:3 NIV

If you get up and do the exact same thing every morning, you may get pretty bored after a month or so. But seeking God when you first wake up is never boring. He will always have a new revelation ready for you to hear.

Keep your expectation fresh by changing what you do in your time with God. You might worship the Lord with singing one morning, listen to Christian music another morning, read God's Word the third morning, sit in His presence or confess His Word the following morning. Let the Holy Spirit lead you as you learn to enjoy starting your day with God.

Form Godly Habits

Fix these words of mine in your hearts and minds . . . talking about them when you sit at home and when you walk along the road, when you lie down and when you get up. Write them on the doorframes of your houses and on your gates, so that your days . . . may be . . . as many as the days that the heavens are above the earth.

DEUTERONOMY 11:18–21 NIV

Waiting for God's direction each day is something you may have to *make* yourself do at first, but through practice, it will become natural to begin your day this way. New habits are formed by being consistent. Seeking God first in the morning will soon be something you can't do without.

When God wanted His people to remember something, He told them to write it down. You may have to post reminders to seek the Lord around your house in order to follow through with your new intention. But be consistent to seek God first every day, and He will make your ways successful (see Joshua 1:7–9).

Crave God's Presence

My soul yearns for You [O Lord] in the night, yes, my spirit within me seeks You earnestly; for [only] when Your judgments are in the earth will the inhabitants of the world learn righteousness (uprightness and right standing with God).

ISAIAH 26:9

If we are hungry enough, we will get something to eat. And if we can't eat before we leave home, we will go to a drive-thru at a fast-food restaurant. Or we will call a place that delivers food to bring us something to eat.

If we are hungry enough for God, we will find a way into His presence. We should be *so hungry* for the presence of God that we absolutely will not go out of our house or tackle any kind of project until we have spent some time with Him.

Don't Be Too Busy

It is because of the Lord's mercy and loving-kindness that we are not consumed, because His [tender] compassions fail not. They are new every morning; great and abundant is Your stability and faithfulness.

LAMENTATIONS 3:22–23

If we are too busy to spend time with God, then we are just too busy, and we are asking for a disaster in our life. We need to ask God to show us things we can get rid of in our life that aren't bearing any fruit.

In His Word God says, "Awake, O sleeper, and arise from the dead, and Christ shall shine (make day dawn) upon you *and* give you light . . . Live purposefully . . . making the very most of the time [buying up each opportunity], because the days are evil" (Ephesians 5:14–16). God wants us to be strong in the power of His might and to be ever filled with the Holy Spirit.

Pray and Listen

Cause me to hear Your loving-kindness in the morning, for on You do I lean and in You do I trust. Cause me to know the way wherein I should walk, for I lift up my inner self to You.

PSALM 143:8

We need to pray and then stop and listen. Sometimes we can hear God as a still, small voice from deep within our heart. Many times God will speak through our inner witness so that we "just know" the truth and it sets us free. Suddenly we know what we should or shouldn't do.

King David had a lot to say about seeking God in the morning. He prayed in the morning and then watched and waited for God to speak to his heart. I like knowing that God is listening for our prayers. He likes it when we listen to His answers too.

Go with What You Know

Satisfy us in the morning with your unfailing
love, that we may sing for joy and
be glad all our days.

PSALM 90:14 NIV

This morning pray, "Lord, I am waiting for You to direct me." While you honor the Lord by listening for His response, you may hear Him speak something specific to you right away. It may seem as though He inscribes direction in your spirit for the day. The devil may tell you that it wasn't really God who spoke to you. Or while you are waiting to hear from God, Satan may tell you that you are wasting your time.

It is important to know the truth of God's Word so that the direction God sows in your heart will not be snatched away from you through doubt. God may not lay out a blueprint for your day, but He *will* direct your path, if you acknowledge Him in all of your ways (see Proverbs 3:6).

Be Happy

The Lord is my Strength and Song; and He has become my Salvation. The voice of rejoicing and salvation is in the tents and private dwellings of the [uncompromisingly] righteous: the right hand of the Lord does valiantly and achieves strength!

PSALM 118:14—15

Happiness is the result of a radical, outrageous relationship with God. If we want to walk in victory, we have to put some time into our relationship with the Lord. There is much to discover about His plans for us.

Our contentment won't last if we are not obeying God by seeking Him with our whole heart. God wants us to really talk to Him and pay attention to His answers. Spend enough time with Him this morning to walk in victory all day.

Give Personal Time

But I say, walk and *live [habitually] in the*
[Holy] Spirit [responsive to and *controlled* and
guided by the Spirit]; then you will certainly not
gratify the cravings and *desires of the flesh*
(of human nature without God).

GALATIANS 5:16

Many believers serve God with their
time, but still miss spending personal
time in His presence. God wants us to *abide* in Him,
not just visit Him occasionally. Jesus said, "If you
abide in My word [hold fast to My teachings and live
in accordance with them], you are truly My disciples" (John 8:31).

Jesus will actually dwell, settle down, abide, and
make His permanent home in your heart! His presence will cause you to be rooted deep in love so that
you may experience His love and be filled through
all your being with the fullness of God (see Ephesians 3:17–19).

Receive By Faith

*I pray You, if I have found favor in Your sight,
show me now Your way, that I may know You
[progressively become more deeply and intimately
acquainted with You, perceiving and recognizing
and understanding more strongly and clearly] and
that I may find favor in Your sight . . . And the
Lord said, My Presence shall go with you,
and I will give you rest.*

EXODUS 33:13—14

Everything that we receive from God comes by faith. When you are waiting for Him to speak to your heart, just believe that He *will* speak to you, even if you don't hear anything right that minute.

Believe that because you have acknowledged Him, you can expect to see His hand moving in your life all day long. Then step forward, knowing that He will keep you on the right path because you have asked Him to do so. Watching God's hand of favor move on our behalf is one of life's greatest delights.

Don't Chase Blessings

*Blessed (happy, fortunate, to be envied) is the man
whom You choose and cause to come near, that he may
dwell in Your courts! We shall be satisfied with the
goodness of Your house, Your holy temple.*

PSALM 65:4

Instead of chasing after blessings, we need
to chase after God. If we chase God, He
will chase us with blessings. That is why the kingdom of God is sometimes called "the upside-down
kingdom."

God's economy doesn't work the way we think
it would. First is last, and last is first. If we want
more, we are to give away some of what we have. To
be great in God's kingdom, we must serve the needs
of others. And if we want blessings, we must get our
mind off of them. God knows what we want and
what we need. He wants to give us blessings that we
haven't even verbally asked for.

Don't Fall Apart

But He said to me, My grace (My favor and loving-kindness and mercy) is enough for you [sufficient against any danger and enables you to bear the trouble manfully]; for My strength and power are made perfect (fulfilled and completed) and show themselves most effective in [your] weakness.

2 CORINTHIANS 12:9

Come apart and spend some time with God before *you* come apart. No matter how strong and healthy you are, no matter what your age is, no matter what you think you know, without God, you are going to get weary and tired.

God doesn't get tired, and the Word says He gives power to the faint *and* weary, and increases strength to those who have no might. But those who wait for the Lord, who expect, look for, and hope in Him, will be renewed (see Isaiah 40:29–31). God is willing to increase your strength. Get alone with Him anytime you need to be strengthened.

Wait for the Lord

Keep the charge of the Lord your God, walk in His ways, keep His statutes, His commandments, His precepts, and His testimonies, as it is written in the Law of Moses, that you may do wisely and prosper in all that you do and wherever you turn.

1 KINGS 2:3

When you pray, wait for the Lord. This means to look for, to expect, and to hope in God. This isn't a passive state of mind, but one of expectancy.

Tell Him, "God, I have my hope in You. I believe that You are working on my problems. I believe that You are making arrangements for my day. You are posting angels all throughout my walk, everywhere along my path where You already know I am going to walk today. Thank you, Lord, that You are a pioneer who has already gone before me and made a way for me to have a blessed day."

Lord, What's Next?

Show me Your ways, O Lord; teach me Your paths.
Guide me in Your truth and faithfulness and teach
me, for You are the God of my salvation; for You
[You only and altogether] do I wait
[expectantly] all the day long.

PSALM 25:4—5

Start your day saying, "I am excited about this day, God. I can hardly wait to see what You are going to do. I believe You are going to keep me, help me, bless me, and give me favor. I love You, Father. I am waiting on You, Lord, and I am listening to You."

Ask God to put into your spirit everything He wants you to know. Ask Him to show you things to come and what you are supposed to do (see John 16:13). He will give you direction, and you will have much to praise Him for today.

Be Renewed

> *God selected . . . what the world calls weak to put the strong to shame. And God also selected (deliberately chose) what in the world is lowborn and insignificant and branded and treated with contempt, even the things that are nothing, that He might depose and bring to nothing the things that are, so that no mortal man should [have pretense for glorying and] boast in the presence of God.*

I CORINTHIANS 1:27–29

If you are weak in faith, in mind, in body, in discipline, in self-control, or in determination, simply wait on God. He will be strong through your weakness.

Isaiah 40:31 teaches that if you expect God, look for Him, and hope in Him, you will change *and* renew your strength *and* power; you will run, and not faint *or* become tired. The Bible doesn't say "hope so, it could be, or it may be"; it declares that you *will* be renewed.

He Will Reward You

So repent (change your mind and purpose);
turn around and return [to God], that your sins may
be erased (blotted out, wiped clean), that times of
refreshing (of recovering from the effects of heat,
of reviving with fresh air) may come from
the presence of the Lord.

ACTS 3:19

Success principles alone will not work in your life if you don't spend time with God, allowing His Holy Spirit to be your Counselor and to give you revelation and understanding of what to do each day. But if you flow in God's plan, you will learn to stop trying to figure out how everything will work together for your good.

Learn to seek God's face and not His hand all the time. Then keep your hands open and be ready to receive from Him. God is good; you can trust what He speaks to your heart to do.

Invert in Someone

The wicked borrow and pay not again [for they may be unable], but the [uncompromisingly] righteous deal kindly and give [for they are able].

PSALM 37:21

Take chances today and invest in someone else's life, especially if God tells you to do so. You may give them something of value only to learn they waste it as they have always done in the past. But remember that God made an investment in you, and He wants you to be willing to make an investment in somebody else.

Jesus died to give *everybody* a chance. Not everyone takes advantage of His provision, but we all have an equal opportunity to enjoy the abundant life. If you help someone, and they end up not doing what is right with it, that is between them and God. Give thanks that you are able to give, and then do whatever God tells you to do.

God Will Keep You

> *[As for me] I am poor and needy, yet the Lord*
> *takes thought and plans for me. You are my Help*
> *and my Deliverer. O my God, do not tarry!*
>
> PSALM 40:17

God has a plan for each of us, and the good things that happen to us are not just a coincidence. All good and perfect gifts come from God (see James 1:17). It is exciting to have a relationship with God when we are aware that He is carefully leading and guiding us to His blessings.

If you don't understand something the first time God speaks to you, He will give you another chance and will continue to teach you until you know clearly the way you should go. Jesus came to seek and to save those who are lost (see Luke 19:10). This means that He will find you if you go astray.

Love God First

Come and see what God has done, how
awesome his works in man's behalf!

PSALM 66:5 NIV

We give attention to whatever we love the most. God wants to be first in our life (see Exodus 20:3). Jesus said, "'Love the Lord your God with all your heart and with all your soul and with all your mind.' This is the first and greatest commandment" (Matthew 22:37–38 NIV).

What might happen in your life if you became so intent on seeking God that you hired a babysitter to watch your children, or used a vacation day, in order to spend time with the Lord? You can't afford *not* to spend time with God. Give Him your full attention, and make a point to observe all He is doing for you.

Confess God's Provision

In conclusion, be strong in the Lord [be empowered
through your union with Him]; draw your strength
from Him [that strength which His
boundless might provides].

EPHESIANS 6:10

When your faith feels weak, ask God to show you how to pray. The Bible says plainly in Jude 1:20–21 and 1 Corinthians 14:2–4 that when you pray in the Holy Spirit, you edify yourself, which means you build yourself up on your most holy faith. Praying in the Holy Spirit causes you to make progress, and His leading will guard *and* keep you full of expectancy and patience for God's mercy to bless your day.

There is no excuse for anybody to drown in doubt and unbelief, when God has given us His Spirit to fill us with faith through prayer and time spent in His presence. Today, start confessing what you have in God. Declare that your needs are met because the Word says so (see Philippians 4:19).

Keep Your Peace

Only fear the Lord and serve Him faithfully
with all your heart; for consider how great are
the things He has done for you.

I SAMUEL 12:24

 To have peace, keep your eyes on God. Get alone to fellowship with Him. If you have to get in a closet and sit in the middle of all your shoes and hang clothes over your head to hide in order to find solitude, do it! Then focus on all that God has done for you.

Jesus said to go to your most private room when you pray to the Father, and He will reward you openly for the time you spend with Him (see Matthew 6:6). Don't miss out on God's abundant blessings for your life.

Prepare to Love Others

The night is far gone and the day is almost here.
Let us then drop (fling away) the works and deeds
of darkness and put on the [full] armor of light.

ROMANS 13:12

Before your feet touch the floor in the morning, put on the full armor of God with which you can quench all the fiery darts of the enemy (see Ephesians 6:13–17). Put on the belt of truth, the breastplate of righteousness, and the readiness of the gospel of peace.

Don't let the devil steal your peace in the morning. Start talking to God before you even get out of bed. Tell Him, "I love You, Lord, and I need Your help today. Please strengthen me to walk in the fruit of the Spirit. Help me walk in love all day long. Help me to keep my thoughts on You, Lord."

Enjoy Confident Trust

In peace I will both lie down and sleep,
for You, Lord, alone make me dwell in
safety and *confident trust.*

PSALM 4:8

Some people feel their lives are an emotional mess, but they have a right to stability. There is stability, peace, and power in the presence of God. People don't have to let their emotions control them; they can learn to dwell in the secret place of the Most High.

The Word says, "HE WHO dwells in the secret place of the Most High shall remain stable *and* fixed under the shadow of the Almighty [Whose power no foe can withstand]. I will say of the Lord, He is my Refuge and my Fortress, my God; on Him I lean *and* rely, *and* in Him I [confidently] trust!" (Psalm 91:1–2).

That is why we should dwell in that place where we experience the presence of the Almighty.

Wait with Purpose

*My [inner] self [as well as my body] is also
exceedingly disturbed and troubled. But You, O Lord,
how long [until You return and speak peace to me]?
Return [to my relief], O Lord, deliver my life; save me
for the sake of Your steadfast love and mercy.*

PSALM 6:3—4

Avoid getting negative when you look at your circumstances. Actively wait on God to give you strength to walk in the fruit of the Spirit (Galatians 5:22—23). Wait with purpose, silently listening for Him to speak, eagerly watching for Him to act.

Tell Him, "Lord, I receive strength to be Your ambassador and witness. Your Word tells me to love people who mistreat me. Though it is hard to do in the natural, I receive strength from You to be loving today."

Then watch for the opportunity to act godly as He gives you strength to do so.

Be Proactive

Have mercy and *be gracious to me; grant*
strength (might and inflexibility to
temptation) to Your servant.

PSALM 86:16

Jesus warned His disciples about all that He was to go through, because He knew it would be difficult for them too. He said, "Pray that you won't be tempted" (see Matthew 6:13; 26:41). He didn't say, "Wait to pray until you have *been* tempted, or until you have *given in* to temptation, or until you are up to your neck in sin and perversion!" Jesus teaches us to be proactive, which Webster defines as "acting in anticipation of future problems, needs, or changes."

Many Israelites had already died from snake bites before the rest of them finally said, "Pray for us, Moses, for we have sinned" (see Numbers 21:4–9). They should have recognized their need for God's help much sooner than they did! Don't wait until you are in trouble to seek God. Ask Him to keep you from being tempted to sin today.

Let God Strengthen You

My life dissolves and *weeps itself away for*
heaviness; raise me up and *strengthen me according*
to [the promises of] Your word. Remove from me the
way of falsehood and *unfaithfulness [to You], and*
graciously impart Your law to me.

PSALM 119:28—29

We need to be strengthened and renewed
on a daily basis. We need to be strengthened physically, mentally, and emotionally. We need
to be strong so we do not fall apart every time we
have to face some situation we had not planned on.

Jesus is the same yesterday, today, and forever,
and He expects us to develop stability in our lives.
We can be strengthened and renewed by drawing
strength from God, by exercising our faith, and by
doing what He tells us to do.

Be Secure

*I love You fervently and devotedly, O Lord, my
Strength. The Lord is my Rock, my Fortress, and my
Deliverer; my God, my keen and firm Strength in
Whom I will trust and take refuge, my Shield, and
the Horn of my salvation, my High Tower.*

PSALM 18:1–2

God can strengthen us to the point that
we can make progress even *during* trouble. The psalmist said of God, "He makes my feet
like hinds' feet [able to stand firmly *or make progress
on the dangerous heights of testing and trouble*] . . .
You have girded me with strength for the battle"
(Psalm 18:33, 39 emphasis mine).

Trials and testing do not come to cause us to
lose stability. They are opportunities to prove the
strength of God. We don't have to waver in our confidence. Nothing will keep us from making progress
today because God is our strength.

Be Strong

The Lord is my Strength and my [impenetrable]
Shield; my heart trusts in, relies on, and confidently
leans on Him, and I am helped; therefore my heart
greatly rejoices, and with my song will I praise Him.
The Lord is their [unyielding] Strength, and He is the
Stronghold of salvation to [me] His anointed.

PSALM 28:7–8

We can plan to be worn out before we ever feel tired. I used to expect to be totally wiped out physically and emotionally after my conferences. Then I prayed that as I poured energy and strength into obeying God, He would pour energy and strength back into me.

The Bible says that giving is sowing a seed that will reap a harvest (Galatians 6:7–10). If we give our strength, we will reap God's strength. We should expect a harvest of strength in our life, as we serve the Lord. He will anoint us with strength today, if we call on Him to do so.

Make Adjustments

*Adding your diligence [to the divine promises],
employ every effort in exercising your faith to
develop virtue (excellence, resolution, Christian
energy), and in [exercising] virtue [develop]
knowledge (intelligence).*

2 PETER 1:5

 Sometimes we have to make a few adjustments in our lifestyle to follow wisdom. We may have to say no to too much activity. Hebrews 11:1 teaches that faith is the assurance of things we do not see now. But, like God, we can call "those things that be not, as though they are" (see Romans 4:17). This spiritual principle applies in the negative realm as well as in the positive realm. So we may need to make some adjustments to the things we say.

If you feel that it is hard to get up in the morning, don't say, "I am too tired." Get all of that weak, tired, wimpy, quitter, give-up talk out of your vocabulary. Instead, say, "Because the Lord is my strength, I can do whatever I need to do today."

God Will Help You

*The Lord will give [unyielding and impenetrable]
strength to His people; the Lord will bless
His people with peace.*

PSALM 29:11

God has been showing me that we need to be aware of His present provisions now, and not in the future. In Psalm 28:7 David said of God, "I am helped; therefore my heart greatly rejoices, and with my song will I praise Him." He did not say, "I *will be* helped."

Wait on God, because God's help will strengthen you to behave in a godly way all day long, if you trust in Him. Even while you wait on God to manifest His plan, your heart can greatly rejoice in His presence. Tell someone something good that God has done for you, and then watch Him move in the presence of your praise.

Offer Yourself Freely

We are the sweet fragrance of Christ
[which exhales] unto God.

2 CORINTHIANS 2:15

The Bible says that every morning God's people brought freewill offerings to Him. They all had various sacrifices such as animals, grains, and cereals (see Exodus 35). God wants us to offer our lives in dedicated service to him.

The Bible says that God is pleased with our sacrifice of praise (see Hebrews 13:15), and that our prayers go up before God as a sweet-smelling sacrifice. He wants us to bring ourselves to Him every morning and say, "God, here I am; I want to be a living sacrifice."

Sacrifice Yourself to Serve

"Give, and it will be given to you. A good measure, pressed down, shaken together and running over, will be poured into your lap. For with the measure you use, it will be measured to you."

LUKE 6:38 NIV

Do you know what Romans 12:1 means when it says that we are to offer ourselves as a living sacrifice? It means that we are to be alive with the power, zeal, and enthusiasm that any born-again person ought to have. It means we are to be excited about Jesus. We are to offer our mouths, our thoughts, our words, our attitudes, our bodies, our hands, and our feet to Him to use to continue His ministry.

This may mean that we do not get everything we want in life, but anything we give up for the sake of the Gospel, Jesus has said we will receive back a hundred times in this lifetime (see Mark 10:29–30). Enjoy God's blessings now. Offer yourself for service and watch the blessings return.

Sacrifice Praise

Know, recognize, and *understand therefore this day and turn your [mind and] heart to it that the Lord is God in the heavens above and upon the earth beneath; there is no other.*

DEUTERONOMY 4:39

Praising God starts your day right. Start thanking God as soon as you get out of bed in the morning. Hebrews 13:15 says, "Let us constantly *and* at all times offer up to God a sacrifice of praise, which is the fruit of lips that thankfully acknowledge *and* confess *and* glorify His name."

Jesus said, "Whoever believes in me, as the Scripture has said, streams of living water will flow from within him" (John 7:38 NIV). Acknowledge the Lord, and drink that living water.

Enter His Gates

You shall [reverently] fear the Lord your God; you shall serve Him and cling to Him, and by His name and presence you shall swear. He is your praise; He is your God, Who has done for you these great and terrible things which your eyes have seen.

DEUTERONOMY 10:20—21

It is not good to feel grumpy when we wake up. Complaining won't bring us into the presence of God. Psalm 100:4 says that we are to enter His gates with thanksgiving and His courts with praise. Without thanksgiving we won't even get into the gate! If we want to enter into God's presence, we must lay aside all murmuring and complaining.

An irritable attitude may be keeping you from enjoying God's presence. Each morning look at all you have to thank God for, and then enter into your day with praise for all He has done for you.

Give Something Away

Yes, the Lord will give what is good, and our land
will yield its increase. Righteousness shall go
before Him and shall make His footsteps
a way in which to walk.

PSALM 85:12—13

God is the ultimate Giver. He expects nothing less than for us to follow His example. I challenge you to give away something every day of your life. You may think you won't have anything left if you do that, but if you give as the Lord leads you to do, soon you will receive so much that you will have to figure out where to put it all.

God gives you bread to eat and seed to sow (see 2 Corinthians 9:10). Some things that God sends your way are given as seed for you to sow into the lives of others. Ask God to show you what He wants you to give away.

Live Unselfishly

The people curse him who holds back grain
[when the public needs it], but a blessing [from God
and man] is upon the head of him who sells it.
He who diligently seeks good seeks [God's] favor.

PROVERBS 11:26—27

I believe strongly in living a "giving life-style." I was selfish for years before I finally realized that joy comes in giving and reaching out to other people. We don't need to be afraid of losing our goods or ending up with nothing, because the Word of God is true.

You will get joyful when you begin to think about how you can bless somebody else. Consecrate your gift to God, saying, "Lord, I give myself to You. I renew my vow, and my commitment to obey You. I want to stay strong in You, so I seek Your face. Bless me, and make me to be a blessing to others."

Bless Somebody

And let us not lose heart and grow weary and faint in acting nobly and doing right, for in due time and at the appointed season we shall reap, if we do not loosen and relax our courage and faint.

GALATIANS 6:9

The Word says, "Let each one of us make it a practice to please (make happy) his neighbor for his good *and* for his true welfare, to edify him [to strengthen him and build him up spiritually]" (Romans 15:2).

This tells me that we need to have our mind *full* of ways to bless people. Early in the day, think up something you want to do to bless someone. Think up something you can do to surprise somebody or to make somebody happy. You will be amazed at how quickly the Lord leads you to something good you can do for someone. Joy comes from giving on His behalf.

Be Honest with God

I will wash my hands in innocence, and go about
Your altar, O Lord, that I may make the voice
of thanksgiving heard and may tell of all
Your wondrous works.

PSALM 26:6–7

Each morning we need to come clean with God. If there is anything between us and God, when we try to pray and get into His presence, it will bother us until we deal honestly with it. God wants us to confess our faults. I have found over the years in a ministry of dealing with other people, and also in dealing with my own flesh, that we don't really like to confront wrongdoing as we should.

Most of us like to make excuses, but excuses keep us deceived. An excuse is a reason stuffed with a lie. The Bible says that the truth will set us free (John 8:32). Honesty with God will free us to enjoy our whole day.

Receive Mercy

All the paths of the Lord are mercy and steadfast love, even truth and faithfulness are they for those who keep His covenant and His testimonies.

PSALM 25:10

The Israelites were lost in the wilderness because they didn't believe that their problems were their own fault. They blamed Moses, God, and everybody else for their sorrows. They refused to take responsibility for their sins, and their unwillingness to repent kept them from entering the promised land.

When you talk with God, be sure to ask for forgiveness. "If we [freely] admit that we have sinned *and* confess our sins, He is faithful and just (true to His own nature and promises) and will forgive our sins [dismiss our lawlessness] and [continuously] cleanse us from all unrighteousness [everything not in conformity to His will in purpose, thought, and action]" (1 John 1:9). Repent in the morning to enjoy God's mercy, forgiveness, and love all day.

Receive God's Gifts

If you are willing and obedient,
you shall eat the good of the land.

ISAIAH 1:19

What good is it to have a glass of water, if we won't drink it? Our thirst will not be quenched until we do. Jesus said, "If any man is thirsty, let him come to Me and drink!" (John 7:37). He said that if we have any kind of need, we are to ask Him for what we want, and then *receive* it. The good things of God are available to those who simply surrender themselves to Him and accept His blessings and mercy.

People beg God for forgiveness but forget to say, "I *receive* that forgiveness right now; I believe I am forgiven." Mercy is a free gift. You can't earn it, you can't deserve it, and you can't buy it. The only thing you can do is *receive* it. Just humble yourself, and accept God's forgiveness.

Abound in Grace

*And God is able to make all grace abound to you,
so that in all things at all times, having all that you
need, you will abound in every good work.*

2 CORINTHIANS 9:8 NIV

My definition of *get* is to obtain by struggle and effort, and *receive* is to act like a receptacle and simply take in what is offered. We can *receive* mercy, grace, strength, forgiveness, and love from the Lord. It is a new day — and God's mercy is new every morning (see Lamentations 3:22–23).

You can have a brand new start today. Allow God's mercy to strengthen and heal you before starting your routine activities. Receive His healing power, and let its grace work in you. Today can be effortless as you depend on God's grace to do what He has called you to do.

Approach God's Throne

*Let us then fearlessly and confidently and boldly
draw near to the throne of grace (the throne of God's
unmerited favor to us sinners), that we may receive
mercy [for our failures] and find grace to help
in good time for every need [appropriate help and
well-timed help, coming just when we need it].*

HEBREWS 4:16

What a great High Priest we have in Jesus. He understands our experiences, and He knows what it is like to live in a human body. He positioned Himself to go through the same kind of temptations we do, but He didn't give in to them.

He knows that the tempter lies in wait for us, and He knows we need His mercy and strength. We still fall short even when we have the best intentions to do good. God tells us to receive, not strive to get, but just to *receive* new mercy for each day.

Be Transformed

But now put away and rid yourselves [completely]
of all these things: anger, rage, bad feeling toward
others, curses and slander, and foulmouthed abuse
and shameful utterances from your lips! . . . And . . .
clothe . . . yourselves with the new [spiritual self],
which is [ever in the process of being] renewed
and remolded into [fuller and more perfect
knowledge upon] knowledge after the image
(the likeness) of Him Who created it.

COLOSSIANS 3:8,10

If you want your life to be different, pray to receive God's transforming power. Simply say:

"God, please forgive my sins and change me into the person You want me to be. I know You are working in me, right now, because I have come to You. You have said that if I abide in Your Word and come into Your presence, I will be changed from glory to glory into Your image. Thank You, Lord, for changing me today."

Believing that God is at work to change you will bring its manifestation.

Simply Believe

We who first hoped in Christ [who first put our confidence in Him have been destined and appointed to] live for the praise of His glory!

EPHESIANS 1:12

In the world, you don't believe anything until you see it. When you pray, believe that you receive, and you will get the manifestation of it. In God's kingdom, you have to believe it first, and then you see it.

Jesus said, "If you believe, you will receive whatever you ask for in prayer" (Matthew 21:22 NIV). God's ear is turned toward those who pray to Him in faith. Peter was the only one who walked on water besides Jesus, but he was also the only one who got out of the boat. Until you make a decision to believe, and then act on it, nothing will happen.

Throw Away Excuses

I will call upon the Lord, Who is to be praised;
so shall I be saved from my enemies.

PSALM 18:3

In Deuteronomy 7:1–2, God instructed His people to utterly destroy their enemies. They were to show no mercy. When God tells us it is time to deal with our negative, faithless attitudes, it is time to throw away our excuses. No more rationalizing, "Well, everybody else is negative; why should I be any different?"

Get some things over with in your life today. Get rid of bad habits and negative attitudes and move on with the future God has for you. Pray: "Lord, please help me to change. Show me the root of my problem and how to get over it. I want positive changes in my life."

Enjoy Forgiveness

Blessed (happy, fortunate, to be envied) is the man
to whom the Lord imputes no iniquity and in
whose spirit there is no deceit.

PSALM 32:2

If we aren't living the way God has instructed us to live, we will be miserable until we confess our sins. Once we thoroughly get everything out in the open before the Lord, He gives us the power to be set free *from* our sins: "BLESSED (HAPPY, fortunate, to be envied) is he who has forgiveness of his transgression continually exercised upon him, whose sin is covered" (Psalm 32:1).

The Word says that God desires truth in our inner being (see Psalm 51:6). So we need to be honest with ourselves and with God, if we want to enjoy the blessing of God's forgiveness. Ask God to show you what needs to be changed in your life, and trust His forgiving power to continually bring about those changes in you.

Seek God Early

And in the morning, long before daylight,
He got up and went out to a deserted place,
and there He prayed.

MARK 1:35

When Jesus told us to *abide* in Him and in His Word, He used the Greek word *meno,* which is translated in Strong's concordance as "continue, dwell, endure, be present, remain, stand, tarry." We are to spend time with God — continually. When we do, we get in the flow of His plan for our day.

We are not told just to *wish* for everything to work together; we are told to *seek God* for a fresh word each day. If we seek Him early in the day, we will have "a word in due season" to share with others (see Proverbs 15:23). We can succeed at what God calls us to do, if we listen for His instructions. He has said, "If you seek Me early and diligently, you will find Me" (see Proverbs 8:17).

Get Alone with God

But when you pray, go into your [most] private
room, and, closing the door, pray to your Father, Who
is in secret; and your Father, Who sees in secret,
will reward you in the open.

MATTHEW 6:6

Jesus rose early to be alone with God, but Peter pursued Him to let Him know that everyone was looking for Him (see Mark 1:35–36). When you get alone to pray, it may seem that everybody tries to hunt you down. But Jesus sought time alone with God so He could focus on His purpose.

We see the scenario of Jesus praying alone and then meeting the needs of others again and again. Jesus went throughout Galilee preaching and driving out demons. When a leper begged to be clean, Jesus touched him, and the leprosy completely left him (see Mark 1:39–42). If Jesus needed to be alone with the Father before He ministered to others, so do we.

Speak God's Mind

*Hear, for I will speak excellent and princely
things; and the opening of my lips
shall be for right things.*

PROVERBS 8:6

One of our biggest mistakes we make is that we sometimes answer people too quickly, just giving them something off the top of our head. Only a fool utters his whole mind (see Proverbs 29:11 KJV). Those who speak frequently and hastily are always in trouble, as the Bible says, "There are those who speak rashly, like the piercing of a sword, but the tongue of the wise brings healing" (Proverbs 12:18).

Jesus operated in wisdom. He always knew just the right thing to say, at just the right moment, to astound everybody. If we don't spend enough time with God, we will say the wrong thing at the wrong time. Decide to wait on God before speaking your mind today.

Be Filled with Truth

Because he has set his love upon Me, therefore will
I deliver him; I will set him on high, because he knows
and understands My name [has a personal knowledge
of My mercy, love, and kindness — trusts and relies
on Me, knowing I will never forsake him, no, never].

PSALM 91:14

Don't let the devil have your thoughts first thing in the morning. Begin early to get your day started right. As soon as you wake up, tell the Lord you love Him. Tell Him you need Him and are depending on Him. Read His Word and confess His promises as you prepare for the day.

Listen to teaching tapes while you are driving to work. Fill yourself with knowledge of God's truth. Don't talk yourself into a disaster before the day even begins. Instead say, "I am the righteousness of God in Christ; because He is with me today, I will rejoice in all things."

Stay in Agreement

*Know the God of your father [have personal knowl-
edge of Him, be acquainted with, and understand
Him; appreciate, heed, and cherish Him] and serve
Him with a blameless heart and a willing mind. For
the Lord searches all hearts and minds and understands all the wanderings of the thoughts. If you seek
Him [inquiring for and of Him and requiring Him
as your first and vital necessity] you will find Him.*

1 CHRONICLES 28:9

God's Word reveals a wonderful plan for your life. It shows how God sees you, and what He has for you through Jesus Christ. Keep your thoughts and words in agreement with God's Word.

Say, "Everything I lay my hand to prospers and succeeds. I am the head and not the tail, above and not beneath. I am blessed going in and going out. The blessings of God chase me down and overtake me. God is on my side. I am blessed to be a blessing to everyone I meet today."

Obey Quickly

Jesus then said to them, I assure you, most solemnly I tell you, Moses did not give you the Bread from heaven [what Moses gave you was not the Bread from heaven], but it is My Father Who gives you the true heavenly Bread.

JOHN 6:32

Jesus said to ask God for *daily* bread (see Matthew 6:11). He also called Himself the "Bread of Life" (see John 6:35). Seek God's direction in the morning to gather His daily words for you. You will feel well nourished all day long. Obey quickly if God tells you to do something.

Even if God gives you a difficult task, don't put it off and dread it all day. Abraham rose early to offer Isaac on the altar; God blessed his obedience and provided an acceptable sacrifice in place of Isaac (see Genesis 22:1–14). David rose up early on the morning that he was to kill Goliath, and through him, God delivered the Israelites from their enemies (see 1 Samuel 17:20–53). He will bless and deliver you too.

Break Free from Bondages

The humble shall see it and be glad; you who seek
God, inquiring for and requiring Him [as your first
need], let your hearts revive and live!

PSALM 69:32

 If it is still hard to start your day right, pray this prayer:

"Lord, I struggle in taking time to fellowship with You and read Your Word. I know that spending time with You is not a law, it is a privilege. It is something that benefits my life. I pray that the bondages, the lies of Satan that keep me out of the prayer closet and away from time with You, will be broken off of me.

"Help me to see clearly that this is something I must do to live in victory. I pray for an anointing that will draw me into Your presence and cause me to run after You. Help me to get every morning started right."

Wake Up with Praise

*My mouth shall praise You with joyful lips when I
remember You upon my bed and meditate on You in
the night watches. For You have been my help.*

PSALM 63:5–7

Many people never have a decent finish
to their day because they let the enemy
keep them from starting it right. Satan tries to capture our thoughts early in the morning. He wants to
get us thinking about all the wrong things as soon as
we wake up. His intent is to steal our peace by upsetting us as soon as our alarm goes off. He is always
working to set us up to get us upset.

That is why it is important to learn how to defeat the devil early each day. Every morning is a new
opportunity to start your day right. Praise God as
soon as your eyes open to a new day.

Cling to God

*My whole being follows hard after You and clings
closely to You; Your right hand upholds me.*

PSALM 63:8

The Word of God has much to say about morning. David started his day praying and listening to God. He instructed the priests to stand every morning to thank and praise the Lord, and likewise at evening. He said "The Lord has given peace *and* rest to His people" (see 1 Chronicles 23:25–30).

Many times we pray and pray, but, like Lot, we don't listen. For example, angels prompted Lot early in the morning to flee from Sodom and avoid its coming destruction (see Genesis 19:15). We can avoid disasters when we wait on God's instructions before acting.

A great beginning leads to a great finish. Begin your day with thanksgiving and praise, and in the evening before you rest, thank the Lord again for a great day.

Answers Will Come

Wait and *hope for* and *expect the Lord;*
be brave and *of good courage and let your*
heart be stout and *enduring.*

PSALM 27:14

I used to wake up wishing it was night, and at night I wished it was morning; I was not enjoying my life. Now I look forward to each day. God arranged life in twenty-four-hour periods; we sleep for a while, and then wake up refreshed to start all over again. God intended every morning to be a brand new start, a fresh opportunity.

We can go to bed feeling hopeless and worn out, thinking, *I just don't believe I can go on.* But somehow a good night's rest renews us, and we wake up with faith again, thinking, *Maybe today my breakthrough will come, and I will get an answer; I can make it one more day.* So thank God for mornings.

Speak Life

Death and life are in the power of the tongue,
and they who indulge in it shall eat the
fruit of it [for death or life].

PROVERBS 18:21

If we ride to work with somebody and gossip about our boss and talk about how we hate our job and what a stupid place it is, we will have a bad day. The Bible says, "A man's [moral] self shall be filled with the fruit of his mouth; and with the consequence of his words he must be satisfied [whether good or evil]" (Proverbs 18:20).

Clearly, we will have to eat our words, so we need to talk about the right things to be happy. If we murmur and gossip, we will eat the fruit of death. But if we speak life, we will eat the fruit of the Spirit (see Matthew 12:37). Choose to eat good fruit today.

Be Prepared

What does the Lord your God require of you but
[reverently] to fear the Lord your God, [that is] to
walk in all His ways, and to love Him, and to serve
the Lord your God with all your [mind and]
heart and with your entire being.

DEUTERONOMY 10:12

Complaining is death, and thanksgiving is life. Yet there are people who complain on their way to church while hoping to receive blessings. They don't understand that complaining keeps them from getting what they want. They don't come prepared to receive blessings in the Lord's presence.

Prepare yourself for blessings by offering thanksgiving for what God has already done for you. The Word says, "For by your words you will be justified *and* acquitted, and by your words you will be condemned *and* sentenced" (Matthew 12:37). Choose your words wisely today, and prepare yourself for God's blessings.

Worship with Your Whole Heart

I will cry to God Most High, Who performs on my
behalf and rewards me [Who brings to pass His
purposes for me and surely completes them]!

PSALM 57:2

Great worship leaders know to come into the presence of God with their entire being, prepared to give thanks and praise (see Deuteronomy 10:12). They don't just roll out of bed, throw water on their face, and run a comb through their hair before church. They know that the anointing comes from a sincere pursuit of loving God with their whole heart.

Likewise, as you approach God in the morning, come to Him with a heart full of worship, expressing your awe of Him for His faithfulness toward you. He promises that He will never forsake you, but will be with you all day long (see Joshua 1:5).

Find Quiet Time

The [reverent] fear of the Lord is clean, enduring forever; the ordinances of the Lord are true and righteous altogether. More to be desired are they than gold, even than much fine gold; they are sweeter also than honey and drippings from the honeycomb.

PSALM 19:9—10

Sometimes I set aside the entire day just to be with God. I stop everything and seek Him. I know I am not going to hear from God if I don't get quiet on purpose by that time set aside for Him.

It is so important to have some "down time" to be alone and just sit quietly. You may think you don't have time, but if somebody was giving out thousand-dollar bills at the mall, you would find time to get there. Don't use the time to try to figure out something; just be still and available to the Lord's attention.

Increase Your Days

*Behold, the Lord's eye is upon those who fear
Him [who revere and worship Him with awe],
who wait for Him and hope in His mercy
and loving-kindness, to deliver them from
death and keep them alive in famine.*

PSALM 33:18—19

When I talk about seeking God early,
many people think they will have to get
up at three o'clock in the morning! I am not trying
to tell you *how* to do it. I am not even suggesting that
you pray for an hour. I am just saying that some way,
somehow, if you want to start your whole day right,
you must find time to seek God's wisdom in the
morning.

Time with God adds years to your life! God is
eager to give us insight and understanding. His Word
says, "For by me [Wisdom from God] your days shall
be multiplied, and the years of your life shall be in-
creased" (Proverbs 9:11).

Refill Your Peace

It is the Lord Who goes before you; He will
[march] with you; He will not fail you or let you go
or forsake you; [let there be no cowardice or flinching,
but] fear not, neither become broken [in spirit]
(depressed, dismayed, and unnerved with alarm).

DEUTERONOMY 31:8

Many times, believers with Christian bumper stickers on their cars are seen driving around like crazy people, yelling at their kids, throwing their hands in the air, and looking mad at the world. If there isn't any peace in our heart when we leave home, our bumper stickers are not going to impress anybody. We need to get ourselves straightened out before we go out.

Pray, "My [inner] self [as well as my body] is also exceedingly disturbed *and* troubled. But You, O Lord, how long [until You return and speak peace to me]?" (Psalm 6:3). Let God refill you with peace.

Put God First

But seek (aim at and strive after) first of all His kingdom and His righteousness (His way of doing and being right), and then all these things taken together will be given you besides.

MATTHEW 6:33

I have learned that spending time with God is a vital necessity in my life. I cannot do what I am called to do if I don't seek the presence of God every day. If I don't have time for God first, nothing else in my life works out.

God isn't happy with second place or third place in our lives.

When we are desperate enough, we find time to seek God. We turn the telephone off, we say no to our friends, and we turn our face away from all distractions and seek Him. That is when we get our breakthrough.

Go to Your Room!

And I have filled him with the Spirit of God,
in wisdom and ability, in understanding and
intelligence, and in knowledge, and
in all kinds of craftsmanship.

EXODUS 31:3

My children didn't like it when I started spending time alone to seek God. They said, "You're always in that room."

One day I told them, "You'd better be glad I am in that room, because it is making your life a whole lot better. If you were smart, you would beg me to go to my room, instead of calling me to come out."

Next time you find yourself screaming, ranting, raving, and carrying on at your children (or anyone else), excuse yourself and say, "I am going to my room." Take time to ask God what He thinks of everything that is going on. You will quickly get your day started over right.

Slow Down

*Peace I leave with you; My [own] peace I now give
and bequeath to you. Not as the world gives do
I give to you. Do not let your hearts be troubled,
neither let them be afraid. [Stop allowing yourselves
to be agitated and disturbed; and do not permit
yourselves to be fearful and intimidated and
cowardly and unsettled.]*

JOHN 14:27

Hurrying affects our spiritual life. Jesus wasn't in a hurry. We can't even picture Him jumping up and saying to His disciples, "Come on, boys, get up. Up, up, up, up! Get this camp meeting cleaned up. Come on, we have to get to the next town. We have some preaching to do. Get the camels packed up, boys. Let's go, let's go!"

When we think about Jesus, we picture peace. He went slow enough to hear from God all day long. We should set our pace with His today.

Turn Down the Noise

*Take My yoke upon you and learn of Me, for I am
gentle (meek) and humble (lowly) in heart, and you
will find rest (relief and ease and refreshment and
recreation and blessed quiet) for your souls.*

MATTHEW 11:29

Noisy people don't hear from God. And
we don't hear from Him when we are
making noise, or when everything around us is
noisy. The only kind of noise you should have in the
morning is my television program; that's all (I am
teasing). But don't turn on the radio or television
just for noise.

Learn how to get comfortable being quiet. The
Bible says, "But whoso hearkens to me [Wisdom] shall
dwell securely *and* in confident trust and shall be
quiet, without fear *or* dread of evil" (Proverbs 1:33).

Linger in God's Presence

Be still and *rest in the Lord; wait for Him* and
patiently lean yourself upon Him.

PSALM 37:7

Sometimes in our conferences, we just "hang out" in God's presence. We sing and worship Him, and soon we enjoy the freshness of His marvelous wonder.

When we sense God is working in people's hearts, we don't worry about our meeting schedule or agenda. We set everything aside to just enjoy His awesome power working among His people. Many who came feeling bad are refreshed, and the sick are healed during this time of worship and waiting on the Lord. It happens all the time — there is healing in God's presence.

If you feel discouraged, He will cheer you up. If you feel tired, He will strengthen you. Just sit in His presence and wait for Him to move in your life.

Focus on God's Promises

For I the Lord your God hold your right hand;
I am the Lord, Who says to you, Fear not;
I will help you!

ISAIAH 41:13

 The Lord says to you this morning the same thing He told Jacob in a dream: "I am with you and will keep (watch over you with care, take notice of) you wherever you may go, and I will bring you back to this land; for I will not leave you until I have done all of which I have told you." (Genesis 28:15). Keep your mind on this promise in spite of any news you may hear that tempts you to be afraid today.

God promises to be with you, watch over you with care, take notice of you wherever you may go, and bring you back again. He says He will not leave you, and He will complete all the promises He has made to you. This means that no weapon formed against you will prosper (see Isaiah 54:17).

Rededicate Yourself

O Lord, [earnestly] remember now how I have walked before You in faithfulness and truth and with a whole heart [entirely devoted to You] and have done what is good in Your sight.

2 KINGS 20:3

"And Jacob awoke from his sleep and he said, Surely the Lord is in this place and I did not know it" (Genesis 28:16). Many times the Lord is with us, and we don't even know it. God is there with you even when circumstances seem out of control. He is already working everything together for your good.

"And Jacob rose early in the morning and took the stone he had put under his head, and he set it up for a pillar (a monument to the vision in his dream), and he poured oil on its top [in dedication]" (v. 18). Likewise, we should rededicate ourselves to God every morning.

Give Your All to God

Before I formed you in the womb I knew [and]
approved of you [as My chosen instrument], and
before you were born I separated and set you apart,
consecrating you; [and] I appointed you as a
prophet to the nations.

JEREMIAH 1:5

Every day you need to give yourself entirely to God. Say, "Lord, I am Yours. I want to be a vessel fit for Your use. I dedicate myself to You: I give You my hands, my mouth, my mind, my body, my money, and my time. Father, here I am. I am Yours; do with me whatever You want to do today."

Once you dedicate yourself to God, then go on about your business. But expect His leading all day long. Listen for His voice to direct you in the way you should go. Accept the challenge to be an instrument for the Lord's use today.

Grasp Every Chance

*I will keep Your law continually, forever and ever
[hearing, receiving, loving, and obeying it].*

PSALM 119:44

You can meet with God while lying in bed. You don't have to be in a private room, with the door closed, bowed down on your knees to meet God. You can meet Him in the shower, while driving to work, or when stuck in a traffic jam.

I am not suggesting that you shouldn't set apart time for God. But you should also take advantage of any time you do have that you could be talking and listening to the Lord. Don't wait to talk to Him until you have a full hour to spend with Him. Grasp every minute you can find to open your ears to His voice. Take advantage of the idle moments already available to you and spend them with God.

Make a Fresh Commitment

Honor the Lord with your capital and sufficiency
[from righteous labors] and with the firstfruits of
all your income; so shall your storage places be
filled with plenty, and your vats shall be
overflowing with new wine.

PROVERBS 3:9—10

The parable of the talents (see Matthew 25:14–30) instructs us to use what God gives to us to expand the Master's kingdom. Invest yourself, your time, and your money in the Lord's work. Rededicate your finances to God today.

Make a fresh commitment to be a giver. Don't let the devil talk you out of giving just because you have bills to pay and obligations that cause you to worry. In Matthew 6:25–34 Jesus said not to be anxious about anything, for God knows your needs and promises to care for you.

Consecrate Your Money

And God is able to make all grace (every favor and earthly blessing) come to you in abundance, so that you may always and under all circumstances and whatever the need be self-sufficient [possessing enough to require no aid or support and furnished in abundance for every good work and charitable donation].

2 CORINTHIANS 9:8

The apostle Paul said that the believers in Macedonia not only gave their money to God, but they also gave themselves to the Lord's service (see 2 Corinthians 8:1–5). Paul too gave his life in service to God's people.

Many people want to receive all they can from God, but they are not willing to give all of themselves to Him. If you have never dedicated yourself to the Lord's service, you are missing a great adventure. Dedicate this day to Him; He will lead you on a path to victory.

Consecrate Your Life

He who brings an offering of praise and *thanksgiving honors* and *glorifies Me; and he who orders his way aright [who prepares the way that I may show him], to him I will demonstrate the salvation of God.*

PSALM 50:23

When I minister to people, I share with them my life and my family. We tell about our victories and our failures. We tell about our mistakes, the stupid things we do, and the wise things we do. We give the testimony of our lives to help others live victoriously too.

Someone needs your life today. Give your life to God, and let Him show you who needs ministry on His behalf. Give Him everything that you are, everything you hope to be, all your dreams, all your visions, all your hopes, and desires. Make everything His, and He will demonstrate His power through your life.

Consecrate Your Mouth

*I have proclaimed glad tidings of righteousness
in the great assembly [tidings of uprightness and
right standing with God]. Behold, I have not
restrained my lips, as You know, O Lord.*

PSALM 40:9

What would happen if every morning we gave our mouth to God so that only godly things came out of our lips? Psalm 34:13 says, "Keep your tongue from evil and your lips from speaking deceit."

Dedicate your mouth to God and use it only for what pleases Him: praise and worship and edification and exhortation and giving thanks. Put your lips on the altar each morning. Give your mouth to God through praying His Word: "O Lord, open my lips, and my mouth shall show forth Your praise" (Psalm 51:15).

Know God Intimately

Rejoice in the Lord always [delight, gladden yourselves in Him]; again I say, Rejoice!

PHILIPPIANS 4:4

In Philippians 3:10 the apostle Paul wrote, "[For my determined purpose is] that I may know Him [that I may progressively become more deeply and intimately acquainted with Him, perceiving and recognizing and understanding the wonders of His Person more strongly and more clearly], and that I may in that same way come to know the power outflowing from His resurrection [which it exerts over believers]."

As you grow in the knowledge of God, you will get so happy you will run the devil right out of your life. Decide that today will be dedicated to recognizing God's power at work in your life. Keep your mind on whatever is right and true and lovely and pure and of a good report (see Philippians 4:8).

Start with Praise

*Through Him, therefore, let us constantly and at
all times offer up to God a sacrifice of praise, which is
the fruit of lips that thankfully acknowledge and
confess and glorify His name.*

HEBREWS 13:15

Moses rose early in the morning, built an altar, and offered burnt offerings and peace offerings to God. Then he prayed and read the Book of the Covenant (see Exodus 24:1–7). Thankfully, God no longer asks us to build an altar out of rocks, slaughter a bull, drain its blood, and build a fire in order to honor Him with a burnt sacrifice.

God doesn't want a dead sacrifice anymore. He wants us, living sacrifices, full of zeal to serve Him each day. All we have to do is wake up and say, "Thank You, Lord. I give You the sacrifice of praise. I give You myself, a living sacrifice, ready to live for You today."

Be God's Ambassador

*And [pray] also for me, that [freedom of]
utterance may be given me, that I may open my
mouth to proclaim boldly the mystery of the good
news (the Gospel), for which I am an ambassador
in a coupling chain [in prison. Pray] that I may
declare it boldly and courageously, as I ought to do.*

EPHESIANS 6:19—20

If you start your day right, you will have
a better day, and you will be a better witness for the Lord. Dedicate yourself to God afresh
each morning.

Tell Him, "Lord, I give You the gifts and talents
that You put in me. I want to use them for Your
glory. I want to lead somebody to You. Put in my
path someone to whom I can minister, someone I
can encourage. Help me to be a blessing to someone
today. Lord, I want to be Your ambassador and rep-
resent You today."

Petition with Thanksgiving

*And God's peace [shall be yours, that tranquil
state of a soul assured of its salvation through Christ,
and so fearing nothing from God and being content
with its earthly lot of whatever sort that is, that
peace] which transcends all understanding shall
garrison and mount guard over your hearts
and minds in Christ Jesus.*

PHILIPPIANS 4:7

We can petition the Lord for things we
need every morning. God's Word tells us
to lay our requests before Him: "Do not fret *or* have
any anxiety about anything, but in every circum-
stance *and* in everything, by prayer and petition
(definite requests), with thanksgiving, continue to
make your wants known to God" (Philippians 4:6).

But don't spend all your time with God petition-
ing for things. You are out of balance if your peti-
tions outweigh your praise and thanksgiving. A heart
full of thankfulness will make any day better.

God Will Brighten Your Day

He set himself to seek God . . . and as long as
he sought (inquired of, yearned for) the Lord,
God made him prosper.

2 CHRONICLES 26:5

Jesus got up early in the morning, long before daylight, and went out to a deserted place, and prayed — He got alone (see Mark 1:35). There were so many people who followed Jesus everywhere He went that He probably wouldn't have had any time alone if He hadn't gotten up really early.

If you aren't a morning person, the thought of getting up early may make you nervous. But you can decipher for yourself what "early" means for you. Nine o'clock is early if you are used to staying in bed until noon. Even if you only get up fifteen minutes earlier than usual to have some time alone with God, you will still honor Him, and that time with Him, will make your whole day brighter.

Enjoy the Pursuit

Blessed (happy, fortunate, to be envied) is he who consider the weak and the poor; the Lord will deliver him in the time of evil and trouble.

PSALM 41:1

Do you ever feel that no matter where you go, somebody pursues you and hunts you down? Does someone seem to need something every time you start doing what you set out to do? Someone needs a ride to school, or somebody forgets their lunch, and before you know it, half your day is wasted.

Jesus knows what it is like to be pursued, but He was never upset by it. As soon as He ministered to everyone in one place, He went to the next town to find more people who needed Him. He never said, "Leave Me alone." Ask God to show you the needs of people through the eyes of Jesus today, and your days will never be wasted.

Prepare for Ministry

*You prepare a table before me in the presence of
my enemies. You anoint my head with oil; my
[brimming] cup runs over. Surely or only goodness,
mercy, and unfailing love shall follow me all the
days of my life, and through the length of my days
the house of the Lord [and His presence]
shall be my dwelling place.*

PSALM 23:5—6

Every day offers opportunities to "be in
ministry." Someone will always need a
helping hand, but you won't minister well if you
don't prepare yourself by spending time with God.
People can tell when you have had intimate moments
with God recently, and also when you haven't.

The Lord anoints us to meet the needs of others,
but if we are not being filled by Him, we will hinder
the flow of His healing oil in our lives. Seek God
early, before someone calls and needs your help.

Operate in Wisdom

*Oh, the depth of the riches and wisdom and
knowledge of God! How unfathomable (inscrutable,
unsearchable) are His judgments (His decisions)!
And how untraceable (mysterious, undiscoverable)
are His ways (His methods, His paths)!*

ROMANS 11:33

Without wisdom we can make poor decisions and later wonder why we didn't pray first. It is wise to seek God early each day before we start making decisions in order to know ahead of time what we ought to do, and then to receive the grace to do it. Wisdom keeps us from a life of regret.

Jesus operated in wisdom. When others went home to rest, Jesus went to the Mount of Olives to spend time with God. And early in the morning (at dawn), He came back into the temple and taught people (see John 7:53–8:2). Jesus always spent time with the Father before facing the crowds. If Jesus needed time with God, we need even more time with Him. Walk in wisdom today.

Realize God's Continual Presence

Though a sinner does evil a hundred times and his days [seemingly] are prolonged [in his wickedness], yet surely I know that it will be well with those who [reverently] fear God, who revere and worship Him, realizing His continual presence.

ECCLESIASTES 8:12

You can form such a habit of prayer that you will wake up in the morning talking to God. You can fall asleep at night talking to God, and wake up in the middle of the night still talking to Him. The Word calls it "prayer without ceasing" (see 2 Timothy 1:3).

I have learned to start my day with prayer and just keep praying all day. I pray when I see somebody hurting. I pray if I don't feel good. I pray when I feel hurried.

Prayer is conversation with God. It is simply being aware of His continual presence and acknowledging Him in all of our ways. If we do, He promises to direct our path to a place of peace and victory (see Proverbs 3:6).

Quit Complaining

Whoso is wise [if there be any truly wise] will
observe and heed these things; and they will
diligently consider the mercy and loving-
kindness of the Lord.

PSALM 107:43

 Today thank God and decide not to complain about anything. Ask Him to show you anytime you are getting ready to complain, and to help you hold your tongue. Today, give thanks for what you have without looking at what you don't have. Some people have the same problems you have, but they don't know God. At least you can give thanks that God is in your life.

The Word says, "Let there be no filthiness (obscenity, indecency) nor foolish *and* sinful (silly and corrupt) talk, nor coarse jesting, which are not fitting *or* becoming; but instead voice your thankfulness [to God]" (Ephesians 5:4). Guard your tongue today.

Pray before Answering

For [of course] I will not venture (presume) to
speak thus of any work except what Christ has
actually done through me [as an instrument in
His hands] to win obedience from the
Gentiles, by word and deed.

ROMANS 15:18

The Father has sent to us a Counselor —
the Spirit of Truth — who teaches us all
things (see John 14:16,17,26). As we stay sensitive
to God's leading, He will direct us. If we pray before
speaking, the Lord will keep us from overcommit-
ting our time, and from misleading people.

Jesus took time to listen to the Father before
speaking. God will also give us "a word in due season" for somebody (see Proverbs 15:23), if we listen for His input before we give what we may think
is a right answer. God will give us the right words to
say if we expectantly listen for His direction before
we speak.

Aim Higher!

Therefore I do not run uncertainly (without definite aim). I do not box like one beating the air and striking without an adversary. But [like a boxer] I buffet my body [handle it roughly, discipline it by hardships] and subdue it, for fear that after proclaiming to others the Gospel and things pertaining to it, I myself should become unfit [not stand the test, be unapproved and rejected as a counterfeit].

I CORINTHIANS 9:26—27

Excessive sleep causes the downfall of many good plans. You can set the clock to get up early and pray, but your flesh is not going to help you get up in the morning. Your body will nearly always beg for more sleep.

Don't let your flesh rob you of time with God. Aim for the higher goal, and wake up with your alarm to enjoy the best minutes of your day.

Start Moving

Bless (affectionately, gratefully praise) the
Lord . . . who satisfies your mouth [your necessity
and desire at your personal age and situation]
with good so that your youth, renewed, is like the
eagle's [strong, overcoming, soaring]!

PSALM 103:1, 5

Proverbs 6:4 says, "Give not [unnecessary] sleep to your eyes, nor slumber to your eyelids." The Bible is saying, "Get the sleep you need, but then wake up!" Too much sleep brings poverty. It is like a robber who steals from you and makes you helpless (see Proverbs 6:11).

Too little sleep will ruin your day too. Being tired and cranky doesn't help you hear from God. Make rest a priority, but then get up. Start moving first thing in the morning, saying, "Thank You, Lord, that I am alive for another day with You. I believe I am anointed to do what You ask me to do today. My youth is renewed like the eagle's, just as You promised."

Love Not Sleep

*My eyes anticipate the night watches and I am
awake before the cry of the watchman, that I may
meditate on Your word.*

PSALM 119:148

It is interesting that our popular greeting is "Good morning." Somewhere along the way, someone realized that if we get started off right in the morning, we will have a good day.

Proverbs 20:13 says, "Love not sleep, lest you come to poverty; open your eyes and you will be satisfied with bread." And Psalm 57:8–9 encourages us to wake up ready to sing praises: "Awake, my glory (my inner self); awake, harp and lyre! I will awake right early [I will awaken the dawn]! I will praise *and* give thanks to You, O Lord, among the peoples; I will sing praises to You among the nations."

Make It a Habit

Besides this you know what [a critical] hour this
is, how it is high time now for you to wake up out
of your sleep (rouse to reality). For salvation
(final deliverance) is nearer to us now than when
we first believed (adhered to, trusted in, and
relied on Christ, the Messiah).

ROMANS 13:11

The Word says that Jesus had a habit of going up the mountain to spend time with God. Luke 22:39 says, "And He came out and went, as was His habit, to the Mount of Olives, and the disciples also followed Him." Jesus formed a habit of communicating with God every morning.

It has been said that if you do something consistently for thirty days, it will become a habit. You can either make or break a habit by consistently doing the same thing. Follow Jesus, and form a habit of starting your day with prayer.

Require God's Presence

*One thing have I asked of the Lord, that will I
seek, inquire for, and [insistently] require: that I may
dwell in the house of the Lord [in His presence] all
the days of my life, to behold and gaze upon the
beauty [the sweet attractiveness and the delightful
loveliness] of the Lord and to meditate, consider,
and inquire in His temple.*

PSALM 27:4

When I first became a Christian, I didn't
desire to pray as much as I do now.
Although I do spend time with God every morning,
I also spend time with Him all day. It seems that I
walk in prayer.

In her powerful book, *Experiencing God through
Prayer*, Madame Guyon says there is a difference between praying *to* God and experiencing Him. At
first you must discipline yourself to pray, but eventually you will give yourself to the ocean of God's
love, and experience His continual presence.

Pray Anywhere

Blessed (happy, fortunate, to be envied) are those
who dwell in Your house and Your presence; they will
be singing Your praises all the day long. Selah
[pause, and calmly think of that]!

PSALM 84:4

Once in the habit of spending time with God, you will miss these encounters if you start your day without talking and listening to Him. You can spend time with God anywhere, while doing anything — in the grocery store, or while cleaning house, for example. I have had great encounters with God while driving my car.

God is always listening for the sound of your voice calling out to Him. Develop a ready ear for His voice too. Whatever you have to do today, do it with the Lord. Acknowledge Him and talk to Him about everything. You will greatly enjoy His company.

Today May Be "One of Those Days"

> *Be alert and on your guard; stand firm in your faith (your conviction respecting man's relationship to God and divine things, keeping the trust and holy fervor born of faith and a part of it). Act like men and be courageous; grow in strength!*
>
> 1 CORINTHIANS 16:13

Have you ever had "one of those days" where nothing went right, yet you were hesitant to pray because you didn't know where God might lead you? God won't always ask you to *do* something; sometimes He just wants to talk to you.

If He does ask you to do something, He will anoint you to do it. You will enjoy the presence of His power, and someone will be blessed by your obedience. Those are the best days of your life. Take time to pray this morning. Today may be "one of those days" that God has a special assignment for you.

Praise God

Enter into His gates with thanksgiving and *a*
thank offering and into His courts with praise!
Be thankful and *say so to Him, bless* and
affectionately praise His name!

There are many opportunities to praise God throughout the day. If thankfulness for your many blessings suddenly rises in your heart, stop right then and tell the Lord how grateful you are for all He has given you.

Say, "I worship You, Lord, for You are worthy to be praised. I need You, and I just want to tell You that I love You. Thank You, Father, for everything."

Then go on with what you are doing as if it is for Him. You will be amazed at how much fun everyday life becomes in the presence of the Lord.

Be Fully Satisfied

Planted in the house of the Lord, they shall flour-
ish in the courts of our God. [Growing in grace] they
shall still bring forth fruit in old age; they shall be
full of sap [of spiritual vitality] and [rich in the]
verdure [of trust, love, and contentment].

PSALM 92:13–14

Many people pursue possessions and awards to satisfy their inner need for contentment. But we can be fully satisfied in lean times and in times of abundance, whether we abase or abound (see Philippians 4:12), when we learn to enjoy fellowship with the Lord as soon as we wake up.

Before you are fully awake, you can start talking to God. Just thank Him for seeing you through yesterday, and for being with you today. Praise Him for providing for you, and for working out all the situations in your life for your good.

Ask Him to make you aware of His presence all day long. Peace fills your heart when your mind is on the Lord. Nothing is more satisfying than walking with God.

Have a Glad Heart

From the fruit of his words a man shall be
satisfied with good, and the work of a man's hands
shall come back to him [as a harvest].

PROVERBS 12:14

I used to live with an ongoing sense of dread until I asked God to show me what was wrong. He spoke the words "evil forebodings," and then showed me His Word concerning this subject: "All the days of the desponding *and* afflicted are made evil [by anxious thoughts and forebodings], but he who has a glad heart has a continual feast [regardless of circumstances]" (Proverbs 15:15).

Anxious thoughts make the day evil. If you expect to have a dismal day, you will be unpleasant yourself. Evil forebodings ruin the day, but faith makes the heart glad and brings miraculous results. If you want to have a good day, raise your expectations to be in line with God's Word.

Don't Dread It

*The hand of the diligent will rule, but the
slothful will be put to forced labor.*

PROVERBS 12:24

Don't spend your day looking for something easy to do instead of tackling the
hard things that need to be done. Do the hard things
first, the ones you dislike the most, and get them out
of the way. For example, don't look at your distaste-
ful jobs and think, *I will do those later.* The hard tasks
will nag at you all day long and drain your energy for
doing the things you want to do.

The spirit of passivity will rob you of productive
energy, but you have the power of God in you to
overcome procrastination. Pray and ask God to help
you finish the tasks you have been dreading. Work
on what is important first, and soon they will no
longer be ruling or ruining your day.

Have Confidence in God

No unbelief or *distrust made him waver
(doubtingly question) concerning the promise of God,
but he grew strong* and *was empowered by faith as he
gave praise* and *glory to God, fully satisfied* and
assured that God was able and *mighty to keep His
word* and *to do what He had promised.*

ROMANS 4:20—21

No one believed David could defeat the giant, but David wasn't discouraged. David had sought the Lord early, which gave him confidence in God to do what he was supposed to do that day. When David killed Goliath, he ran quickly to the battlefield and proclaimed victory in the name of the living God (see 1 Samuel 17:20—54).

People who rise early and seek God go forth to do what they must do with courage. Ask God for confidence to slay any giants in your life that have set themselves against God's plan for you.

Be a Blessing

You will guard him and keep him in perfect and constant peace whose mind [both its inclination and its character] is stayed on You, because he commits himself to You, leans on You, and hopes confidently in You.

ISAIAH 26:3

Galatians 6:10 says, "Be mindful to be a blessing, especially to those of the household of faith." Second Corinthians 10:5 speaks of casting down imaginations and every high and lofty thing that exalts itself against the knowledge of God. In other words, keep (set) your mind on God's promises and on what is relevant to His plan for your life.

Don't let your mind be taken captive by the enemy. Instead, "lead every thought and purpose away captive into the obedience of Christ." Decide to be a blessing to everyone you meet today. Forgive anyone who has hurt you, and leave unresolved circumstances in God's hands. Don't use today to relive yesterday. Say, "I am moving forward today, in Jesus' name."

God Gives Us All We Need

*And they who know Your name [who have
experience and acquaintance with Your mercy]
will lean on and confidently put their trust in You,
for You, Lord, have not forsaken those who seek
(inquire of and for) You [on the authority of God's
Word and the right of their necessity].*

PSALM 9:10

In His Word God has given us the tools
we need to help us through each new day.
He has given us "the garment of praise for the spirit
of heaviness" (Isaiah 61:3 KJV). So, when you wake
up in the morning, decide that no matter what happens, you will not be depressed today.

Put on the garment of praise first thing in the
morning. Listen to worshipful music, read the Word,
and renew your thoughts to bring them into line with
what God says you are — righteous and blessed. You
can think right, talk right, and act right all day, if you
spend time with God before trials come your way.

Some Things Never Happen

*You will show me the path of life; in Your
presence is fullness of joy, at Your right hand
there are pleasures forevermore.*

PSALM 16:11

Many times we get upset about things
that never happen. Satan likes to get us
anxious about things that are not even real problems. Jesus said, "The thief comes only in order to
steal and kill and destroy. I came that they may have
and enjoy life, and have it in abundance (to the full,
till it overflows)" (John 10:10).

The Bible says that the kingdom of God is internal righteousness, peace, and joy in the Holy Ghost
(see Romans 14:17). When we make Jesus Lord of
our heart, we have joy in our lives. Satan has no right
to steal from you today, so enjoy the good life that
Jesus paid for you to have.

Love Yourself

*Keep out of debt and owe no man anything,
except to love one another; for he who loves his
neighbor [who practices loving others] has fulfilled
the Law [relating to one's fellowmen, meeting
all its requirements].*

ROMANS 13:8

Jesus said, "Love your neighbor *as your-self*" (see Matthew 18:19). So we need a healthy respect for ourself if we want to enjoy our relationships with other people. If we don't have a balanced love for ourselves, it is difficult to love others. Life is no fun if we can't enjoy other people, because they are everywhere we go!

Sometimes it is difficult to get along with people because they seem so different from us, but it is our differences that make us need one another. God designed us to need each other's friendships and talents. Do something nice for someone today. Let someone know that you appreciate him or her.

Get Along with Others

But the meek [in the end] shall inherit the earth and shall delight themselves in the abundance of peace.

PSALM 37:11

We can *learn* to get along with people. It is especially important to learn to get along with our immediate family members and co-workers. There are many informative books about personality differences to help us understand why people feel and act the way they do. Understanding helps to smooth over strained relationships.

People make decisions differently. Some give an immediate answer, while others want time to think about things first. Try to understand the people you will see today. Ask God to show you ways to get along with them. He will give you favor as you trust in Him.

Positive Change

Bear (endure, carry) one another's burdens and
troublesome moral faults, and in this way fulfill and
observe perfectly the law of Christ (the Messiah)
and complete what is lacking [in
your obedience to it].

GALATIANS 6:2

Our happiness and joy are not dependent on whether or not other people do what we want them to do. We may never be able to influence anyone else to do what we think is right. But with God's help, we can change ourselves to bring about the results we want in life.

I have discovered that if I change in a positive way, and if it is a permanent and stable change, it almost always provokes change in the people around me. If you want your life to be different, ask God to show you how *you* need to change. Accept others for who they are, and see how God works in you to complete your joy.

Live to Full Potential

For you are becoming progressively acquainted
with and recognizing more strongly and clearly the
grace of our Lord Jesus Christ (His kindness, His
gracious generosity, His undeserved favor and
spiritual blessing), [in] that though He was [so very]
rich, yet for your sakes He became [so very] poor,
in order that by His poverty you might become
enriched (abundantly supplied).

2 CORINTHIANS 8:9

I used to wake up feeling guilty and condemned. I was full of judgment and criticism for every little mistake I made. But that outlook creates pressure inside of us that is apt to explode in the face of the first person who comes around.

If you struggle this way, begin your day by reading the Word. Knowledge of God's mercy and forgiveness is vital in learning to love yourself so that you can love others. Live today to its fullest potential.

A Useful Vessel

*So whoever cleanses himself [from what is ignoble
and unclean, who separates himself from contact with
contaminating and corrupting influences] will [then
himself] be a vessel set apart and useful for honorable
and noble purposes, consecrated and profitable to the
Master, fit and ready for any good work.*

2 TIMOTHY 2:21

The Bible refers to us as earthen vessels
(see 2 Corinthians 4:7); we are made of
clay (see Isaiah 64:8). God formed Adam out of
the dirt (see Genesis 2:7), and King David said,
"Remember Lord, that I am but dust" (see Psalm
103:14).

When we fill ourselves with God's Word, we become containers of His blessing, ready to be poured
out for His use. God can even use cracked pots! We
are all valuable to the Lord. We can offer His truth
to people everywhere we go.

Read God's Word before you go about your routine today, and see how many people you can bless
with the truth of His love.

Show Jesus

*And become useful and helpful and kind to one
another, tenderhearted (compassionate, understanding, loving-hearted), forgiving one another [readily
and freely], as God in Christ forgave you.*

EPHESIANS 4:32

I hope to show to everyone I meet the character of Jesus through my words and actions. I pray that everyone who contacts our ministry team will say: "Those people are full of Jesus. They are patient, kind, and sweet."

We are containers capable of being filled to overflowing with the Spirit of Jesus, who dwells in our hearts. If we understand that everywhere we go we can demonstrate His character and virtue, we will be as the Word says — lights in a dark world (see Philippians 2:15).

Jesus called us the salt of the earth (see Matthew 5:13). Salt gives flavor to what is otherwise bland or tasteless. Be salt today — at home, at your job, wherever you go.

Stay Plugged In

*Let your light so shine before men that they may
see your moral excellence and your praiseworthy,
noble, and good deeds and recognize and honor and
praise and glorify your Father Who is in heaven.*

MATTHEW 5:16

Jesus is the Light of the world and He lights up those who come into relationship with Him. When Moses spent time in God's presence, his face became so bright that he wore a veil because people feared to come near him (see Exodus 34:29–30).

As a lamp must be plugged into the electrical outlet to illuminate the darkness around it, so we must stay plugged into God if we want our light to shine before others. The only way we can walk in love and behave the way we should is to pray, read the Word, and experience fellowship with God. Stay plugged in, and be a light wherever you go.

Don't Get Upset

May He grant you out of the rich treasury of His glory to be strengthened and reinforced with mighty power in the inner man by the [Holy] Spirit [Himself indwelling your innermost being and personality].

EPHESIANS 3:16

The devil sets us up to get upset so that we act ugly, throw fits, and ruin our witness of what God has done in our lives. Without God's love flowing through us, it is hard to be nice to nice people, let alone to treat difficult people nicely. We need God's help to live well.

The Holy Spirit will give you the power to walk in love everywhere you go. Don't leave home without inviting Him to fill you with the grace to demonstrate God's love and compassion toward everyone you meet.

Really Come to Know God

[I pray] that you may be filled [through all your being] unto all the fullness of God [may have the richest measure of the divine Presence, and become a body wholly filled and flooded with God Himself]!

EPHESIANS 3:19

Paul was praying for us (the church) when he said, "I pray that you might really come to know, practically and experientially for yourselves, the love of Christ, which far surpasses mere knowledge without experience" (see Ephesians 3:19). He knew that we needed to experience the love of God personally.

Our faith is not dependent on experiences, but our relationship with God *is* real, and we can expect visitations from God. We need times of God's outpouring in which we know, without a doubt, that He is moving in our lives.

Begin the journey of getting to know God better and better. Be aware of His love for you all day.

Desire More of God

I pray You, if I have found favor in Your sight,
show me now Your way, that I may know You
[progressively become more deeply and intimately
acquainted with You, perceiving and recognizing and
understanding more strongly and clearly] and that
I may find favor in Your sight. And [Lord, do]
consider that this nation is Your people.

EXODUS 33:13

As you get to know God better, you will undergo a transition from just praying during times of trouble to wanting to serve Him with everything you are, every breath you take, and every talent you possess. When you fall in love with Jesus, you will crave more and more time with Him.

Once you offer your time, your money, and your gifts to the Lord, you will want to spend every day getting to know Him more intimately. Ask God to fill your entire being with His fullness as you seek Him with all of your heart.

Be Filled with God

*My mouth shall be filled with Your praise
and with Your honor all the day.*

PSALM 71:8

Consider again the verse from Ephesians 3:19: "That you may be . . . a body wholly filled and flooded with God Himself!" Imagine what your day will be like if your body is *wholly filled* with God. You will be a container, carrying God everywhere you go. It will affect your thoughts, emotions, and actions. Being filled with the divine presence of God will change what you say, the entertainment you choose, and the people with whom you elect to spend time.

When we are born again, Jesus comes to live in us as a seed. Caring for that seed of new life by watering it with the Word, nurturing it through direction, and weeding out the sins in our lives makes the seed of His presence grow bigger and bigger until it fills our entire being.

Bearing Fruit

You have not chosen Me, but I have chosen you
and I have appointed you [I have planted you], that
you might go and bear fruit and keep on bearing,
and that your fruit may be lasting [that it may
remain, abide], so that whatever you ask the Father
in My Name [as presenting all that I AM],
He may give it to you.

JOHN 15:16

The Bible says that we are blessed if our confidence is in the Lord. We will be like trees planted by the waters that continue to bear fruit (see Jeremiah 17:7–8).

I admit that sometimes, at the end of a day, we may feel that all of our fruit has been picked! But God will replenish us if we abide in Him. If we put our trust in God, we will bear all kinds of fruit, and will have new fruit to share with others every morning.

Use the Keys

They who seek (inquire of and require) the Lord
[by right of their need and on the authority of His
Word], none of them shall lack any beneficial thing.

PSALM 34:10

Jesus said, "I will give you the keys of the kingdom of heaven; and whatever you bind (declare to be improper and unlawful) on earth must be what is already bound in heaven; and whatever you loose (declare lawful) on earth must be what is already loosed in heaven" (Matthew 16:19).

As a believer, you have authority to live a life of victory and to forbid the devil to torment you. It is not lawful for him to destroy you in heaven, so it is not lawful for him to destroy you during your days on earth. Use the keys of the kingdom of heaven that Jesus has passed to you. Loose God's blessings upon your efforts and bind the evil works that come against the fruit of your labors today.

Brokenness Is Good

Show Your marvelous loving-kindness, O You Who
save by Your right hand those who trust and take
refuge in You from those who rise up against them.
Keep and guard me as the pupil of Your eye;
hide me in the shadow of Your wings.

PSALM 17:7—8

David said, "Lord, I am like a broken vessel" (see Psalm 31:12). Brokenness seems bad, but through brokenness we rid ourselves of the outer shell, the fleshly parts of us, that need to be thrown off in order to bring forth the good things that are in us.

All of us need to be broken as David was; we need to be totally dependent on God to deliver us from evil. Pray today as David did: "But I trusted in, relied on, *and* was confident in You, O Lord; I said, You are my God" (Psalm 31:14).

Broken and Poured Out

For the Son of Man is going to come in the glory
(majesty, splendor) of His Father with His angels, and
then He will render account and reward every man
in accordance with what he has done.

Be willing to give your best to the Lord, and He will use your gifts in ways beyond your imagination. The lady with the alabaster jar of perfume that was worth a year's wages wanted to do something for Jesus because she loved Him. So she poured out the expensive perfume on Him, not realizing at the time that she was anointing Him for His burial (see Mark 14:1–9).

God led her to give what she had, no matter how costly. As you pour out the gifts God has given you, He will use them to prepare the world for the second coming of His son. Your obedience today will reap rewards in heaven that you are not aware of now.

Bless People

For you, brethren, were [indeed] called to freedom;
only [do not let your] freedom be an incentive to your
flesh and an opportunity or excuse [for selfishness],
but through love you should serve one another.

GALATIANS 5:13

As a believer in Jesus Christ, you have wonderful, wonderful gifts on the inside of you. You have the ability to make others happy today. You can encourage. You can edify. You can exhort and uplift. You can believe. You can pray. You can lead somebody else to Christ.

People don't have to have desperate needs before we bless them. The Holy Spirit will lead us to be good to people every day, if we will be sensitive to His voice. Offer your gifts and talents to the Lord, and see what happens.

Do Good

This message is most trustworthy . . . so that those who have believed in (trusted in, relied on) God may be careful to apply themselves to honorable occupations and *to doing good, for such things are [not only] excellent* and *right [in themselves], but [they are] good* and *profitable for the people.*

TITUS 3:8

What an awesome thing it is to be good to people. The Bible says that God anointed Jesus with the Holy Spirit and with strength, ability, and power; and that He went about doing good, for God was with Him (see Acts 10:38). Jesus spent His days being good to people — all people. He helped and encouraged people everywhere He went.

We are anointed to bless people as Jesus did. God has given us the strength, ability, and power to do awesome works in His name. Do good all day — today.

Humble Yourself

Let this same attitude and *purpose* and *[humble]*
mind be in you which was in Christ Jesus: [Let Him
be your example in humility].

PHILIPPIANS 2:5

Humility comes from brokenness; brokenness hurts so bad, but it "hurts good." Brokenness comes when we learn that we are not hotshots after all. Brokenness comes when we judge others, and then realize that we do the same things they do. Brokenness comes when we think *we are* going to step out and do something great, and then fall flat on our face because we forgot to stay plugged in to God.

Brokenness comes when we give our opinion, knowing that we are absolutely right to the point of arguing about it, and then find that we are wrong. Brokenness is good for us. Brokenness leads to humility, and humility precedes honor (see Proverbs 15:33).

Let God Be Exalted

The proud looks of man shall be brought low, and
the haughtiness of men shall be humbled; and the
Lord alone shall be exalted in that day.

ISAIAH 2:11

None of us are where we need to be, but, thank God, we are not where we used to be. Don't look at what you are *going through* right now; look at the person you are *becoming*. We are always in the process of becoming like Christ (see 2 Corinthians 3:18).

Brokenness hurts, but the alternative is much worse. The Word says, "Haughtiness comes before disaster, but humility before honor" (Proverbs 18:12). Pray to be bendable, pliable, and moldable so that you will be more like Christ in all that you do today. Pray to be broken so that the Lord may be exalted in your life.

A Precious Treasure

All these [gifts, achievements, abilities] are
inspired and brought to pass by one and the same
[Holy] Spirit, Who apportions to each person
individually [exactly] as He chooses.

1 CORINTHIANS 12:11

In 2 Corinthians 4:7, Paul says, "We possess this precious treasure [the divine
Light of the Gospel] in [frail, human] vessels of
earth, that the grandeur *and* exceeding greatness of
the power may be shown to be from God and not
from ourselves." God uses frail people (cracked
pots!) to proclaim the power of His gospel.

He could send angels to preach the gospel, but
He uses plain, ordinary, everyday people to demonstrate His power. He fills us with divine gifts, inspired and brought to pass by the Holy Spirit, and
distributes them throughout His body of believers.
Let us network with God's people today for the
greater good, as we work together to accomplish
His purpose.

It Must Be God

For You cause my lamp to be lighted and *to shine;*
the Lord my God illumines my darkness.

PSALM 18:28

The Bible says that God works through our weakness so that the grandeur and exceeding greatness of the power in our lives may be shown to be from Him and not from ourselves (see 2 Corinthians 4:7). God uses ordinary people like us with flaws and cracks in our pots (our earthen vessels), so that people will know that it has to be God working in us if we are doing good works.

If people knew us before we trusted in Jesus, they especially notice the difference that a few years of walking with the Lord has made in our lives. We become totally different creatures when we allow His love to shine through our weaknesses. We may look the same, but we don't act the same. We just ooze with love when we are filled with God's exceeding greatness. Let His glorious light shine through you all day.

Light Shines Through Cracked Pots

Let not those who wait and hope and look for You,
O Lord of hosts, be put to shame through me; let not
those who seek and inquire for and require You
[as their vital necessity] be brought to confusion
and dishonor through me, O God of Israel.

PSALM 69:6

Everyone is like a pot that carries life. But not everyone carries a presence that blesses others. Religion tries to force people to follow laws to make them perfect, like pots without cracks. But if a light is put within a flawless pot and then covered, no one is able to see the light inside the pot. Perfect pots are not able to reveal internal light to illumine the way for others.

God chooses to shine through imperfect, cracked pots. People are blessed when our cracked pots let the light of Jesus shine through. Choose to be a glory-filled, cracked pot rather than an empty, pretty vessel.

Die to Sin

*And Peter answered them, Repent (change your
views and purpose to accept the will of God in your
inner selves instead of rejecting it) and be baptized,
every one of you, in the name of Jesus Christ for the
forgiveness of and release from your sins; and you
shall receive the gift of the Holy Spirit.*

ACTS 2:38

Dying to sin requires a daily commitment. We all have weaknesses, but that is why we need Jesus. He would have died for us in vain if we didn't need Him. Each day we must ask Him to help us with our problems and our flaws.

He will save us from our sins, tempers, selfishness, jealousy, and greed. When we become Christians, our fleshly desire to sin doesn't die *in* us, but Jesus will save us *from* our sins if we ask Him for strength to die to selfish desires and follow Him.

Identify Who You Are

*Let him turn away from wickedness and shun it,
and let him do right. Let him search for peace
(harmony; undisturbedness from fears, agitating
passions, and moral conflicts) and seek it eagerly.
[Do not merely desire peaceful relations with God,
with your fellowmen, and with yourself, but
pursue, go after them!]*

I PETER 3:11

Paul said, "I want to do what is right, but I can't" (see Romans 7:15–25). He was a new person on the inside because he was born again, but he still had to resist the temptation to sin.

Paul explained that "the sin [principle]" (v. 20) continues to dwell in us. We want to do right, but we don't have the power to perform it, because evil is ever present to tempt us to do wrong. Only God can deliver us from this tendency to sin; that is why we must ask Him to deliver us from evil each day.

Enlarge Your Circle of Love

Behold, how good and how pleasant it is
for brethren to dwell together in unity!

PSALM 133:1

We can dress up and look pretty on the outside, but God is more concerned about what is going on inside us. When we judge others by the way they look, we fall into the devil's trap of rejecting everyone who does not appear to be like us.

Purposely enlarge your circle of love today. Seek ways to include others you may have previously overlooked. Ask God to help you enlarge your circle of love by taking in people of all types, colors, and backgrounds. Pray for eyes to see into people's heart, and expect to enjoy a great day.

We Need Each Other

Again I tell you, if two of you on earth agree
(harmonize together, make a symphony together)
about whatever [anything and everything] they may
ask, it will come to pass and be done for them by
My Father in heaven.

MATTHEW 18:19

We need each other in the body of Christ. Men and women need each other — denominations need each other. I believe that when we get to heaven, we will learn the truth about our differences. We will learn that all of us were right about some things and wrong about others.

But even the things we were right about won't matter. God wants us to get along, to stop fighting with everyone over petty things we disagree about, and to begin to find the things we can agree about so that we may get along with one another. Practice looking for ways to agree with other believers, and then watch what God does through the unity of faith.

Christ Is the Power

And God also selected (deliberately chose) what in the world is lowborn and insignificant and branded and treated with contempt, . . . so that no mortal man should [have pretense for glorying and] boast in the presence of God.

I CORINTHIANS 1:28–29

"But to those who are called, . . . Christ [is] the Power of God and the Wisdom of God" (1 Corinthians 1:24). When God calls us to do something, He enables us to do it. Remember, God uses inadequate people to do important things because that way He gets the glory.

So if God calls you to do something today that seems too big for you to handle, Christ will give you the power and the wisdom that you need to do it. God has said to each of us, "*My* strength *and* power are made perfect (fulfilled and completed) *and show themselves most effective* in [your] weakness" (2 Corinthians 12:9).

God Uses What Others Throw Away

And the Lord said to him, Who has made man's mouth? Or who makes the dumb, or the deaf, or the seeing, or the blind? Is it not I, the Lord? Now therefore go, and I will be with your mouth and will teach you what you shall say.

EXODUS 4:11—12

God purposely calls people to serve Him who don't know how to do what He tells them to do. His tool chest is full of weak individuals who can't seem to do things right, "cracked pots" whom the world treats with contempt (1 Corinthians 1:28).

But God knows that these individuals will depend on Him and will pray, "Lord, help me," "so that no mortal man should [have pretense for glorying and] boast in the presence of God" (1 Corinthians 1:29).

Qualify yourself for God's tool chest today by telling someone what you have seen God do in your life.

God Enables Us

*It is through Him that we have received grace
(God's unmerited favor) and [our] apostleship to
promote obedience to the faith and make disciples for
His name's sake among all the nations, and this
includes you, called of Jesus Christ and invited
[as you are] to belong to Him.*

ROMANS 1:5–6

God gives us beauty for ashes, the oil of joy for mourning, and the garment of praise for the spirit of heaviness (see Isaiah 61:3). God gives us whatever we need to be victorious. Because He enables us, we credit Him for all the good things in our lives.

Get up today and do the best you can, and then let God do the rest. Don't try to make mistakes, don't try to fail; but when you do, repent and get things straight with God. If you need to apologize to somebody, go and apologize. Receive your forgiveness, and go on.

Grow Continually

For this reason, since the day we heard about you,
we have not stopped praying for you and asking God
to fill you with the knowledge of his will through all
spiritual wisdom and understanding. And we pray
this in order that you may live a life worthy of the
Lord and may please him in every way: bearing fruit
in every good work, growing in the knowledge of God.

COLOSSIANS 1:9—10 NIV

God's Word encourages us to strive for perfection by growing into complete maturity of godliness in mind and character, having integrity, as our heavenly Father is perfect (see Matthew 5:48).

Paul said that even though he had not attained the ideal of perfection, he pressed on to grasp and make his own that for which Christ had laid hold of him (see Philippians 3:12). We, too, should press toward maturity and integrity today.

Repent, and Move On

*If we [freely] admit that we have sinned and
confess our sins, He is faithful and just (true to His
own nature and promises) and will forgive our sins
[dismiss our lawlessness] and [continuously] cleanse
us from all unrighteousness [everything not in conformity to His will in purpose, thought, and action].*

1 JOHN 1:9

It is important to be sincerely sorry if we
do something wrong, but it doesn't help
anybody for us to openly mourn over everything
that is wrong with us. We will never mature in our
faith if we stay angry at ourselves.

We are to repent of our sin, receive forgiveness
of it, and then forget it. We must not drag memories
of our old behavior around with us all the time.
Sooner or later we have to let go and say, "Well, I
made a mistake because I am just an old cracked
pot." Then we must let God's light shine through the
holes in our surface.

God Wants Your Heart

But the Lord said to Samuel, Look not on his
appearance or at the height of his stature, for I have
rejected him. For the Lord sees not as man sees;
for man looks on the outward appearance,
but the Lord looks on the heart.

1 SAMUEL 16:7

Religious teaching turns our attention to our outward appearance, but it doesn't empower us to clean up our inside thoughts and intentions. Jesus called the religious Pharisees "whitewashed tombs full of dead man's bones" (see Matthew 23:27), because they boasted of their perfect obedience to the Hebrew laws.

But God didn't see them as perfect, because their hearts were not merciful as is His. God would rather have someone with a sweet, wonderful heart toward Him, who makes mistakes, than somebody with a slick performance, who is rotten inside.

When God looks at your heart today, let Him find it wholly seeking Him.

God Likes the Way He Made You

My frame was not hidden from You when I was being formed in secret [and] intricately and curiously wrought [as if embroidered with various colors] in the depths of the earth [a region of darkness and mystery].

PSALM 139:15

Have you ever asked God, "Why did You make me this way?" Sometimes the things that we think are our worst faults, God will use to His greatest glory: "But who are you, a mere man, to criticize *and* contradict *and* answer back to God? Will what is formed say to him that formed it, Why have you made me thus?" (Romans 9:20).

Jesus died so that we might enjoy our life in abundance and to the fullest until it overflows. You are not going to enjoy your life if you don't enjoy yourself. Be satisfied with yourself, and celebrate the unique way God made you.

Live to Serve God

For even the Son of Man came not to have
service rendered to Him, but to serve, and to give
His life as a ransom for (instead of) many.

MARK 10:45

As the potter forms clay into vessels, some for honorable use and some for menial use, so God forms us to serve His purpose. Regardless of how our position in life may look to others, we are all formed to serve the Lord in some way.

If God made you to be a helper, then help with all your heart. If you enjoy cleaning houses for people, then do so as if you are cleaning the Lord's house. If you want to stay home with your children instead of earning extra income, don't worry that God has called others to paying positions outside the home. Do whatever the Lord puts in your heart to do — and enjoy fulfilling your God-given purpose.

Only God Can Change You

The Lord will sustain, refresh, and *strengthen him
on his bed of languishing; all his bed You [O Lord]
will turn, change,* and *transform in his illness. I said,
Lord, be merciful* and *gracious to me; heal my inner
self, for I have sinned against You.*

PSALM 41:3—4

Don't obsess over your faults, or you will never enjoy the life that Jesus died to give you. Only God can change you, so talk to Him about your desires. The Word says that those who wait on the Lord will *change* (see Isaiah 40:31).

Meanwhile, quit taking your flaws so seriously. Don't let discouragement or depression rob you of your energy and make you angry. If you do, you may take that anger out on other people and miss the blessings God has in store for you today. Enjoy yourself, and lighten up! Take the right steps today toward the change you want to make by asking God to help you all day long.

We Are Carriers

The Lord make His face to shine upon and enlighten you and be gracious (kind, merciful, and giving favor) to you; the Lord lift up His [approving] countenance upon you and give you peace (tranquility of heart and life continually).

NUMBERS 6:25—26

Looking at seemingly successful people and thinking, *Oh, I wish I was like them,* wastes much time. We don't know their problems or their flaws. Everyone has trials, and we should thank God for our own, because if we didn't have problems, we wouldn't need Jesus anymore.

Reveal to others the glory of God's presence in your life by being grateful for what He is doing for you. Understand that God puts His treasures in earthen vessels, like us, so that those who don't know Him will see His grandeur and glory in us (see 2 Corinthians 4:7). Let the light of God shine through your life today.

In Our Weakness
He Is Strong

Yes, You are my Rock and my Fortress; therefore
for Your name's sake lead me and guide me.

PSALM 31:3

Each of us has our own unique flaws, like cracked pots. But if we will allow it, Jesus will use our flaws to grace His Father's table. In God's great economy, nothing goes to waste.

So as we seek ways to minister together and as God calls you to the tasks He has appointed for you, don't be afraid of your flaws. Acknowledge them and allow Him to take advantage of them so that you too can be a thing of beauty in His pathway.

Go out boldly, knowing that in our weaknesses we will always find His strength. In Christ the answer to every one of His promises is "Yes," and for this reason we say, "Amen, so be it!" (see 2 Corinthians 1:20).

His Strength Is Perfect

And [God] Who provides seed for the sower and bread for eating will also provide and multiply your [resources for] sowing and increase the fruits of your righteousness [which manifests itself in active goodness, kindness, and charity].

2 CORINTHIANS 9:10

There are people who have a lot, but who do nothing for others with what they have. And there are people who have little, but who are able to do much with what they have. Use what you have today, and don't worry about what you don't have. God will make up the difference of what you lack, if you will just give Him what you can.

God's strength is always made perfect in your weaknesses. Don't apologize for your shortcomings; instead, watch for God's presence to fill your void. Be the best that you can possibly be, and enjoy the glory God receives through your testimony every single day.

Decide to Be Positive

For the rest, brethren, whatever is true, whatever is worthy of reverence and is honorable and seemly, whatever is just, whatever is pure, whatever is lovely and lovable, whatever is kind and winsome and gracious, if there is any virtue and excellence, if there is anything worthy of praise, think on and weigh and take account of these things [fix your minds on them].

PHILIPPIANS 4:8

Negative people don't enjoy life. Viewing each day with positive expectations is one of the key principles to godly happiness.

We act on what we believe, so positive thoughts cause positive actions. If you want a positive life, begin thinking positive thoughts. It is easy to do so if you read the Word and meditate on all that God wants to do for you and through you. Get alone today, and think about all the good, positive things God has done for you in the past, and all He has planned for you in the future.

Bless Someone Today

In everything I have pointed out to you [by example] that, by working diligently in this manner, we ought to assist the weak, being mindful of the words of the Lord Jesus, how He Himself said, It is more blessed (makes one happier and more to be envied) to give than to receive.

ACTS 20:35

To have a healthy love walk today, spend time this morning thinking about what you can do for somebody else. Don't wait for God to *ask* you to do something; take the initiative and say, "Okay God, what can *I* do to be a blessing on Your behalf today?"

The best days you live are the ones you spend loving other people. Choose a particular person, and think about ways to bless him or her. If you don't know what to do, just listen to what he or she says, and before long you will hear of that individual's needs.

God Knows and Sees

The secret [of the sweet, satisfying companionship]
of the Lord have they who fear (revere and worship)
Him, and He will show them His covenant and
reveal to them its [deep, inner] meaning.

PSALM 25:14

Nobody else may see the things you do, but God sees them all. Every time you pray, God sees it. Every time you do an act of kindness secretly, God sees it and plans a reward to give you openly (see Matthew 6:1–6).

Serve the Lord in all that you do today. The Word says, "In the morning sow your seed, and in the evening withhold not your hands, for you know not which shall prosper, whether this or that, or whether both alike will be good" (Ecclesiastes 11:6). God will prosper what you do for Him.

You Can Change

*We were buried therefore with Him by the baptism
into death, so that just as Christ was raised from the
dead by the glorious [power] of the Father, so we too
might [habitually] live and behave in newness of life.*

ROMANS 6:4

You will never reach your destiny by thinking negative thoughts. When you first wake up in the morning, start saying, "I love my life. It is wonderful. I thank God for everything He has given me."

You will do yourself a favor if you start thinking right thoughts so that you will also choose right actions. Sowing the right actions into your day will form new habits. As you begin to operate in those new habits, you will change in your character. And as your character changes, you will move into the destiny that God has for you. By God's power you can live in newness of life.

Enjoy Challenges

*But it is good for me to draw near to God; I
have put my trust in the Lord God and made Him
my refuge, that I may tell of all Your works.*

PSALM 73:28

Another key to starting your day right is not to dread things. Don't lie in bed dreading the whole day before you even get up. Dread is a close relative of the spirit of fear. When dread enters, joy leaves. Dread sets you up for misery, because by choosing to dread you decide that you cannot enjoy what you must do today.

Be excited when you face new tests. Close the door to the mindset of dread. Decide early to enjoy every challenge that faces you today, knowing that God will be with you to make your path straight and to prosper in everything you set out to do.

Have a New Mindset

Create in me a clean heart, O God, and renew a right, persevering, and steadfast spirit within me.

PSALM 51:10

We set ourselves up either for misery or for joy by the mindset that we have toward the things in our life. Mindsets are the patterns in which our mind normally operates toward a certain determination. For example, when we look at our schedule today, it may seem that there is far too much to do. But if we choose the mindset that God will help us through it, we will enjoy watching how everything falls into place.

Refuse to dread what must be done. Greet the day with a right attitude and a thankful heart that you have a Savior who is ready to rescue you from more than you can handle. Enjoy yourself and say, "I refuse to live in dread; I am going to enjoy my life today."

Perfect Love Casts Out Fear

I have strength for all things in Christ Who
empowers me [I am ready for anything and equal to
anything through Him Who infuses inner strength
into me; I am self-sufficient in Christ's sufficiency].

PHILIPPIANS 4:13

Dread is a relative of fear. The devil tempts us with dread to get us to confess fear instead of faith. But 1 John 4:18 says, "There is no fear in love [dread does not exist], but full-grown (complete, perfect) love turns fear out of doors *and* expels every trace of terror! For fear brings with it the thought of punishment, and [so] he who is afraid has not reached the full maturity of love [is not yet grown into love's complete perfection]."

Enjoy your day, knowing that God loves you perfectly. Don't dread the hard things that you must do today, because God is on your side and is ready to help you.

God Is on Your Side

For the Lord takes pleasure in His people; He will beautify the humble with salvation and adorn the wretched with victory.

PSALM 149:4

If you never face trials, you will never have to exercise your faith. But even when facing hard times, you shouldn't dread life. Isaiah 8:13 says, "The Lord of hosts — regard Him as holy *and* honor His holy name [by regarding Him as your only hope of safety], and let Him be your fear and let Him be your dread [lest you offend Him by your fear of man and distrust of Him]."

If you dread life and fear people, you are not trusting the Lord to save you. Keep your reverential fear and awe of God; dread displeasing Him, but don't fear anything else. If God is for you, who can be against you? "No, in all these things we are more than conquerors through him who loved us" (Romans 8:37 NIV).

Be Ready

Forsake not [Wisdom], and she will keep, defend,
and protect you; love her, and she will guard you.

PROVERBS 4:6

Philippians 4:13 promises that Christ will empower you for anything you must face. This means that He will make you ready for anything and equal to all challenges by infusing you with inner strength.

God will never put you in a position to do something without giving you the strength and the ability to do it. You can relax and enjoy your life, for God will "strengthen (complete, perfect) *and* make you what you ought to be *and* equip you with everything good that you may carry out His will; [while He Himself] works in you *and* accomplishes that which is pleasing in His sight, through Jesus Christ" (Hebrews 13:21).

Renew Your Joy

Honor and majesty are [found] in His presence;
strength and joy are [found] in His sanctuary.

Emotional trauma drains people of their energy. But the Word says, "Be not grieved *and* depressed, for the joy of the Lord is your strength *and* stronghold" (Nehemiah 8:10). The devil wants to steal your joy because he knows that joy is your strength. He wants you to be weak so that you won't resist the turmoil he sets against you. That is why sometimes we need each other.

Some days God will send messengers to build you up in faith and renew your joy. Some days He will send you to someone else who is in a weakened condition because Satan has been pounding on them. Be someone's friend today. They may need a friend to stand beside them and encourage them and to lift them up and pray for them.

Think Ahead

But rather what we are setting forth is a wisdom
of God once hidden [from the human understanding]
and now revealed to us by God — [that wisdom]
which God devised and decreed before the ages
for our glorification [to lift us into the
glory of His presence].

1 CORINTHIANS 2:7

Look ahead to the reward God has for you in heaven. God has already written the end of the Book which says that good news is in store for those who put their faith in Jesus.

Even if you live to be a hundred years old, and have trials every day of your life, Paul said that our momentary troubles are achieving for us an eternal glory that far outweighs all the trials we face now (see 2 Corinthians 4:17–18 NIV). Keep your eyes on the finish line and not on the turmoil around you.

Be Satisfied

The poor and afflicted shall eat and be satisfied;
they shall praise the Lord — they who [diligently]
seek for, inquire of and for Him, and require Him
[as their greatest need]. May your hearts be
quickened now and forever!

PSALM 22:26

Many people constantly seek the thrill of a new experience, but every new thing eventually becomes an old thing. Sooner or later, people have to be happy with old things too, or they will never reach God's higher goal of contentment (see 1 Timothy 6:6).

In Philippians 4:11–12, Paul said that he had learned how to be content and satisfied to the point where he wasn't disturbed or disquieted, no matter what state he was in. He could live in humble circumstances or enjoy plenty. He had learned that the secret of facing every situation, whether well-fed or hungry, was to be content. Seek contentment in God today, and you will be satisfied.

Enjoy Your Life

*Whatever may be your task, work at it heartily
(from the soul), as [something done] for the Lord and
not for men, knowing [with all certainty] that it is
from the Lord [and not from men] that you will
receive the inheritance which is your [real] reward.*

COLOSSIANS 3:23

Jesus died so that you can enjoy abundant life, not just the days you are off work or on vacation or when you get to go shopping or golfing — but every day of your life.

He wants you to enjoy going to the grocery store. He wants you to enjoy driving the kids to school. He wants you to enjoy paying the bills. He wants you to enjoy cleaning the house or mowing the yard.

You can enjoy life if you determine to do so. Say, "I am going to enjoy every aspect of my life, because Jesus died so that I could have joy unspeakable and full of glory."

Follow God's Spirit

And He Who searches the hearts of men knows what is in the mind of the [Holy] Spirit [what His intent is], because the Spirit intercedes and pleads [before God] in behalf of the saints according to and in harmony with God's will.

ROMANS 8:27

Many people follow their own desires or other people's advice instead of following the Spirit of God. The Holy Spirit is given to each one of us to lead us into the fullness of our destiny, and into the fullness of what Jesus died to give us.

Your faith in Jesus gives you the promise of heaven, but God wants to work all things together for your good in this life too (see Romans 8:28). Don't be satisfied with receiving half of what Jesus died to give you. Follow the Spirit's leading so that you will get all that God has for you. Seek God for clear guidance to remain right in the center of His perfect will for every single day.

Go Where God Sends You

*Let us all come forward and draw near with true
(honest and sincere) hearts in unqualified assurance
and absolute conviction engendered by faith (by
that leaning of the entire human personality on God
in absolute trust and confidence in His power,
wisdom, and goodness).*

HEBREWS 10:22

One of the main reasons people don't enjoy their lives is that they don't follow the leading of the Holy Spirit. Because Jesus fulfilled the law, we have full freedom to enter into the Holy of Holies and fellowship with the Father. Hebrews calls this "a fresh (new) and living way" to enjoy our relationship with God (see Hebrews 10:20).

Spend time with God today, and go wherever the Spirit of God leads you. He will always give you the grace to do what He calls you to do.

A New Desire

For I endorse and *delight in the Law of God in my inmost self [with my new nature].*

ROMANS 7:22

When we are born again, we get a new "want to." The law says we "have to, should, and ought to," but we want to do the right thing because God has put a new heart in us to replace the hard stony one that used to be indifferent to Him and His will (see Ezekiel 36:26).

Learn to recognize the difference between the desires of your flesh and the desires placed in you by the Holy Spirit. Psalm 1:1–2 says, "BLESSED (HAPPY, fortunate, prosperous, and enviable) is the man who walks *and* lives not in the counsel of the ungodly . . . But his delight *and* desire are in the law of the Lord, and on His law (the precepts, the instructions, the teachings of God) he habitually meditates (ponders and studies) by day and by night."

Everyone Is Different

*Having gifts (faculties, talents, qualities) that
differ according to the grace given us, let us use them.*

ROMANS 12:6

Don't feel bad about yourself if you are
not able to do what someone else is
anointed to do. God anoints each of us to contribute
to the body of Christ in some unique way. What
God enables you to do is no more or less important
than what He has called someone else to do.

God made you different from everyone else to
fulfill the desire of His heart, and He promises to fulfill the desires of your heart too (see Psalm 37:4).
He will anoint whatever He's given you, so place
your gifts in His power today, and enjoy yourself.

Change "Must" to "Want"

Therefore, [there is] now no condemnation (no adjudging guilty of wrong) for those who are in Christ Jesus, who live [and] walk not after the dictates of the flesh, but after the dictates of the Spirit.

ROMANS 8:1

Many of us compare ourselves and our achievements to others and what they accomplish for the Lord, thinking we *have to* do certain things to please God. But God didn't send Jesus into the world to condemn us (see John 3:17). What pleases God most is our deep craving to know Him better, which is achieved by spending time with Him through study and prayer.

We are called to enjoy fellowship with God. Don't let condemnation rob you of your joy today. Pray: *Lord, I want to follow the law of my new being. By Your grace, help me follow Jesus, because He has done what the law could not do and has saved me from my sins.*

Follow Peace

Now the mind of the flesh [which is sense and reason without the Holy Spirit] is death [death that comprises all the miseries arising from sin, both here and hereafter]. But the mind of the [Holy] Spirit is life and [soul] peace [both now and forever].

ROMANS 8:6

People hesitate to follow their desires, because they don't know how to divide their soul from their spirit. If they can't discern the difference between the desires of their flesh and Spirit-led desires, then they don't know when God is truly leading them to do something.

But you can learn to know if God is leading you or not. When God gives you a desire for something, He will give you peace along with it. You may not be excited, but you will have peace, if the thing you desire is from God. Wait for peace today.

Recognize Your Calling

*That is why I would remind you to stir up
(rekindle the embers of, fan the flame of, and keep
burning) the [gracious] gift of God, [the
inner fire] that is in you.*

2 TIMOTHY 1:6

Before I knew I was called to preach, I would privately repreach entire sermons I had just heard, thinking, *I would have said this, and, I would have done that.* Then, I would think, *Women don't preach!* But my spirit was stirred by the preacher's anointing because I had the same anointing.

If you are called to do something, you will get stirred up in the presence of someone operating in that same anointing. For example, if you have an anointing to lead worship, or to do special music, you will probably get more excited about the music than the sermon being preached. When in doubt, ask God to make clear your calling.

Iron Sharpens Iron

Iron sharpens iron; so a man sharpens the countenance of his friend [to show rage or worthy purpose].

PROVERBS 27:17

If you want to do something for God, then don't associate with people who do nothing. You may have to drastically change your life if you want to move on with what God has called you to do. Spend time with people who know how to use their days well.

Just as iron sharpens iron, positive people will inspire you to be positive. Godly people will inspire you to use your faith to do for the Lord what is in your heart to do. Spend time with people who are doing something for the Lord. Elisha got a double portion of Elijah's anointing, but he had to associate with Elijah for a long time to get it (see 2 Kings 2:1–14).

Follow Your Heart's Desires

Who is the man who reverently fears and worships the Lord? Him shall He teach in the way that he should choose. He himself shall dwell at ease, and his offspring shall inherit the land.

PSALM 25:12—13

To enjoy your life, start following the God-given desires of your heart instead of the desires of your flesh. You may need to mature in faith before you can tell the difference between your flesh and Spirit-led desires.

One way to tell if you are following a desire of your flesh is that when you step out to do it, you will lose your peace and face a struggle. If it is not of God, you will feel like you are pushing a dead horse uphill. If it is a God-given desire of the Spirit, it will work like a well-oiled machine. It will flow, with what I call a "Holy ease." Start your day right, and follow your heart.

Get Peace from God

If any of you is deficient in wisdom, let him ask of the giving God [Who gives] to everyone liberally and ungrudgingly, without reproaching or faultfinding, and it will be given him.

JAMES 1:5

Be careful when somebody makes a suggestion that sounds good; not every good idea is a God-idea. Don't rush into making a decision or accepting a new responsibility without praying about it first.

Slow down long enough to ask God for wisdom, and listen for His guidance. Take a little bit of time to see if you have peace about the idea. If you don't have peace, you don't even have to understand *why* you don't have peace. Just don't do it!

Quality Is Better than Quantity

I call to remembrance my song in the night; with my heart I meditate and my spirit searches diligently.

PSALM 77:6

God cares more about the quality of what you learn than the quantity of teaching to which you are exposed. He would rather you read one scripture verse and get revelation out of it than to read two whole books in the Bible and not have a clue about what you read.

Listen for key messages that the Lord is specifically speaking to you when you hear good teaching through television, radio, sermon tapes, a church service, or weekly Bible study. Ask God to show you how to apply what you hear to your own life. Meditate on His Word each day and look for ways to use what you have learned. Then you will know that you are engaging in and enjoying true quality time with Him.

Study Daily

Practice and *cultivate* and *meditate upon these duties; throw yourself wholly into them [as your ministry], so that your progress may be evident to everybody.*

1 TIMOTHY 4:15

Second Timothy 2:15 says, "Study *and* be eager *and* do your utmost to present yourself to God approved (tested by trial), a workman who has no cause to be ashamed, correctly analyzing *and* accurately dividing [rightly handling and skillfully teaching] the Word of Truth."

It is difficult to grow if you don't like to read the Word. If Satan has created obstacles to keep you from reading the Word, take authority over him. Declare your love for the Word, and then read it — even if only a couple of pages a day. Your desire for more will quickly increase. If you truly don't like to read, then pray that God will give you a brand new desire to do so right now.

Choose How to Live

For it is by free grace (God's unmerited favor) that you are saved (delivered from judgment and made partakers of Christ's salvation) through [your] faith. And this [salvation] is not of yourselves [of your own doing, it came not through your own striving], but it is the gift of God.

EPHESIANS 2:8

You can live under the law of sin and death, with its rules and regulations; or you can live under the law of the Spirit of life in Christ Jesus, which by grace sets you free from the law of sin and death (see Romans 8:2).

Galatians 5:4–5 explains that the law brings us to nothing and separates us from Christ. But the Holy Spirit will help us conform to God's will in purpose, thought, and action. Choose the law of life and say, "Today I will enjoy a grace-filled day."

Let God Lead Others

*Yes, let none who trust and wait hopefully and
look for You be put to shame or be disappointed; let
them be ashamed who forsake the right or deal
treacherously without cause.*

PSALM 25:3

Our day might seem better if everyone would just do what we tell them to do. But God doesn't override people's will, and we are not to do so either. Instead of trying to control people, pray that they will "hear" God leading them.

If someone persists in doing something his or her own way today, show your confidence in God by stepping aside. You may learn that you were wrong, or they may learn that you were right. God is big enough to get both you and them out of any mess they may make. Either way, He will get the glory, if you put your trust in Him.

Don't Be Afraid to Stop

The thoughts and *purposes of the [consistently]*
righteous are honest and *reliable, but the counsels*
and *designs of the wicked are treacherous.*

Don't be ashamed to back off if you get
out in the middle of something and find
that God is not in it. Just be secure enough to simply
say, "I thought this was God, but it's not, so I am not
going to do it anymore."

You can apologize to others if you caused them
any trouble or confusion. But there is no shame in
quickly admitting that you were wrong. It is more
important not to perpetuate a mistake than it is to
keep people from thinking you were wrong. Don't
be afraid to say, "I didn't hear from God." Honesty
will keep your day going right, all day long.

Wait for Peace

A man's mind plans his way, but the Lord
directs his steps and makes them sure.

PROVERBS 16:9

You may have to step out to find out the right thing to do. If you don't hear clearly from God, just step in the direction you think you should go, and then wait for peace. If you lose your peace, back out of wherever you were headed.

Dave and I almost bought two different buildings to house our ministry. We were in negotiations until, one morning after praying, Dave said, "Joyce, I don't have peace about buying that building. I feel like God is saying, 'If you buy that building, you are going to be sorry later.'" So we waited for peace, and now we have a building that is completely paid for with room to grow. Pray until you find peace.

Follow God's Leading

Roll your works upon the Lord [commit and trust them wholly to Him; He will cause your thoughts to become agreeable to His will, and] so shall your plans be established and succeed.

PROVERBS 16:3

Trying to figure everything out before you obey God will steal your joy. God doesn't have to answer you when you ask, "Why God, why?" Trust means that you won't always have answers when you want them. Sometimes you just have to get to the other side of a situation to see the whole picture of what God is doing in your life.

God may be trying to separate you from some influence in your life that is keeping you from receiving the better plan He has for you. He may be "pruning" you to encourage new, healthier growth (see John 15:1–8). Use uncertain times to demonstrate your faith by trusting Him.

Let Disappointments Go

*But he who keeps (treasures) His Word [who bears
in mind His precepts, who observes His message in its
entirety], truly in him has the love of and for God
been perfected (completed, reached maturity).*

1 JOHN 2:5

It can be disappointing when people who are close to us don't do what we would like for them to do. But if we really love them, we should encourage them to follow the Holy Spirit rather than try to keep us happy all the time.

Help others grow spiritually by encouraging them to listen for God's voice. Remind them that God will help them through mistakes and lead them to a good life. Soon they will be making Spirit-led, rather than people-led, decisions. It is tremendously gratifying to see loved ones mature spiritually in Christ.

The Law of the Spirit

*Behold, God, my salvation! I will trust and not be
afraid, for the Lord God is my strength and song;
yes, He has become my salvation.*

ISAIAH 12:2

Life is not just one long party; there will
always be hard things and easy things
mixed together in the events of your life. Regardless
of what today brings, you can still have joy in the
Lord, and that joy will give you strength to handle
whatever comes your way on any given day.

When you follow Jesus, the law of the Spirit of
life keeps you free to enjoy yourself because you can
cast any burdens on the Lord (see Romans 8:2).
God will lead you to know what to do, and He will
energize you to do what needs to be done. You
won't feel drained by life, but will grow through
both the trials and the triumphs as you walk with
God today.

Do Whatever God Says

So that the righteous and just requirement of the
Law might be fully met in us who live and move not
in the ways of the flesh but in the ways of the
Spirit [our lives governed not by the standards
and according to the dictates of the flesh,
but controlled by the Holy Spirit].

ROMANS 8:4

"In Him we live and move and have our being" (Acts 17:28). God is everything. Talk to Him all day long, every time you need to make a decision or overcome anything negative. Whatever He says to do, do it. If He says don't do it, don't do it. You don't belong to yourself; you belong to God.

Religious teaching tries to predetermine what God wants from you. But He will write on your heart what is good and what is bad for you to do. He will speak to your inner conscience and keep you safe, as long as you pay attention to His voice and do what He tells you. Throughout the day today, occasionally stop what you are doing and ask Him if there is anything He wants to say to you.

Love Is the Higher Law

Love does no wrong to one's neighbor [it never hurts anybody]. Therefore love meets all the requirements and is the fulfilling of the Law.

ROMANS 13:10

There are things that we shouldn't do, simply because we love God, and because we don't want to hurt somebody else's conscience. We may have the freedom to do these things, but our freedom could offend others, or cause them to do something against their conscience, and thus sin against God.

If you walk in love today, there may be things that you have the right to do, but the Holy Spirit will prompt you not to exercise your right out of love for someone who is watching you. Love never demands its own way (see 1 Corinthians 13:5). Love is always the higher law.

Wear the Right Armor

And all this assembly shall know that the Lord
saves not with sword and spear; for the
battle is the Lord's.

1 SAMUEL 17:47

When David went out to face Goliath, everyone around him said, "David, you can't do this!" But God put a sense of "knowing" within David that he would succeed in the name of the Lord. When King Saul decided to let David fight, he gave David his armor, but David said, "I cannot, because I am not used to this" (see 1 Samuel 17:31–39). David *knew* he was to go in the name of the Lord with only his slingshot (see vv. 40–50).

If you have battles to face in life, don't let others tell you how to fight. God will personally direct you in the way you should go. His Word is your weapon; that is why it is a vital necessity to arm yourself with knowledge and to spend time in God's presence before you have to face any giants.

God's Plan Is Greater

*For the law of the Spirit of life [which is]
in Christ Jesus [the law of our new being] has
freed me from the law of sin and of death.*

ROMANS 8:2

The law of the Spirit of life in Christ Jesus sets us free from the law of sin and death. We are free from the law of sin and death only to the degree that we follow the law of the Spirit. If we know what is right but insist on doing wrong, our actions may still lead us to miss out on the abundant life God has for us on earth.

Follow the law of the Spirit, and you will remain completely free from the law of sin and death. The Holy Spirit will lead you into holiness, into righteousness, and into the complete destiny that God has for your life. God's will for you is greater than anything you can imagine for yourself. Be willing to obey God even when you don't understand what He is doing with you.

Follow God's Priorities

The sheep that are My own hear and are listening
to My voice; and I know them, and they follow Me.

JOHN 10:27

Many people try to feel spiritual by obeying religious laws. But they never get around to feeling good, because there is always one more law to follow. That is why God does not define our righteousness by our works, but by our faith in Jesus. We feel inner peace when we obey the voice of the Holy Spirit.

God may tell you that it is more important to give away your favorite personal possession, than to try to please Him by reading the Bible through in a year. He may say that it is more important to just remain silent, if He tells you to, than to volunteer for every activity at church. His ways are not our ways (see Isaiah 55:8–9), so learn to listen for His direction each day.

Have Fun

For the kingdom of God is not a matter of eating and drinking, but of righteousness, peace and joy in the Holy Spirit, because anyone who serves Christ in this way is pleasing to God and approved by men. Let us therefore make every effort to do what leads to peace and to mutual edification.

ROMANS 14:17–19 NIV

Everything in your life doesn't have to be serious in order to be spiritual. If you are filled with God's Spirit, whatever you do has a spiritual connotation to it. You can live a holy life, and still enjoy your day.

God measures holiness by how quick we are to obey His voice. He promises that goodness and mercy will follow us if we seek His presence (see Psalm 23:6). He may even encourage you just to have fun today.

Pamper Yourself

Why are you cast down, O my inner self? And why should you moan over me and be disquieted within me? Hope in God and wait expectantly for Him, for I shall yet praise Him, my Help and my God.

PSALM 42:5

God gave you your emotions, so it doesn't work to ignore them completely. You make a big mistake if you refuse to meet any of your emotional needs. If you are tired, you need rest. If you are stressed, you need some fun.

If you need encouragement, spend time with someone who knows how to build you up. Don't ignore your emotional needs in the name of Christianity. You are a whole person — body, soul, and spirit (see 1 Thessalonians 5:23). God will show you how to be strong in all areas of your life.

Set Priorities

Your eyes saw my unformed substance, and in Your book all the days [of my life] were written before ever they took shape, when as yet there was none of them.

PSALM 139:16

Be *determined* to enjoy the abundant life that Jesus Christ desires for you to have. The devil will always try to set you up to get upset. The busy activities of today's society can make life seem like a blur. Most people have a lot of stress, continuous pressure, and really too much to do.

Set priorities. Start your day with God. Be determined to follow His lead all day, and you will enjoy every day of your life — not just on weekends, vacations, or sunny days when the weather's perfect. Walking with God will give you pleasure and relaxation even when things aren't going your way.

Clean Up

Let us throw off everything that hinders and the
sin that so easily entangles, and let us run with perse-
verance the race marked out for us. Let us fix our eyes
on Jesus, the author and perfecter of our faith.

HEBREWS 12:1–2 NIV

Have you ever gone on a cleaning rampage to straighten up your home or office? Did you enjoy pitching junk, straightening objects, and organizing materials so that you could find them when you need them?

You may need to get on a Holy Ghost rampage and do the same thing with your life. Say, "I've had enough bondage. I've had enough negative thoughts. I've had enough of the lies of the devil. I am not going to have any more bad days. I am not going to be discouraged, depressed, or despondent. I am going to enjoy my life!"

Jesus is ready to help you live life to the fullest!

Joy Unspeakable

*Now to Him Who is able to keep you without
stumbling or slipping or falling, and to present
[you] unblemished (blameless and faultless) before
the presence of His glory in triumphant joy and
exultation [with unspeakable, ecstatic delight].*

JUDE 1:24

I used to be so miserable when I went to
bed that I wished it was time to get up.
And when I got up, I was still so miserable I wanted
to go back to bed. I was under the curse of not obeying the voice of the Lord or serving Him with joy-
fulness (see Deuteronomy 28:15–48).

Obedience to God fills our lives with so much
joy that we don't even know how to talk about it.
The Bible calls it "joy unspeakable and full of glory"
(1 Peter 1:8 KJV). Experience the joy of being in
God's awesome presence. Start your day by praising
God for your blessings, and worshiping Him with a
heart ready to serve Him.

The Key to Joy

And may the God of peace Himself sanctify you through and through [separate you from profane things, make you pure and wholly consecrated to God]; and may your spirit and soul and body be preserved sound and complete [and found] blameless at the coming of our Lord Jesus Christ (the Messiah).

1 THESSALONIANS 5:23

Righteousness is a key to enjoying every single day of your life. Being in right relationship with God is available to us simply through our faith in Jesus Christ. That security gives us peace through every situation, and having peace brings joy.

The Word says to listen with expectancy to what God the Lord will say to you, for He will speak peace to His saints (those who are in right standing with Him), and those who don't turn again to self-confident folly (see Psalm 85:8). Before making plans today, listen for God's voice to make sure you follow His peace for your day.

The Key to Loving Others

Now may the Lord of peace Himself grant you
His peace (the peace of His kingdom) at all times
and in all ways [under all circumstances and
conditions, whatever comes].

2 THESSALONIANS 3:16

The Bible says to love your neighbor as yourself (Luke 10:27); the key is to love yourself. You won't enjoy your day until you learn to accept and enjoy yourself, because you have to eat with yourself, sleep with yourself, and be with yourself all day. Until you are happy with who you are and where you are in life, you will never learn to love others or get to where you want to be.

Don't get down on yourself about everything you didn't do right yesterday. Today is a new day. Learn to love your life, right now, right where you are now. Say, "I am grateful to be a child of God, redeemed and made righteous in His eyes. I am going to enjoy myself all day long."

No Matter What

*For you shall go out [from the spiritual exile
caused by sin and evil into the homeland] with joy
and be led forth [by your Leader, the Lord Himself,
and His word] with peace; the mountains and the
hills shall break forth before you into singing, and all
the trees of the field shall clap their hands.*

ISAIAH 55:12

Peace is not dependent on circumstances.
Our peace and joy are found in *the Holy
Ghost*. Jesus said:

He who believes in Me [who cleaves to *and*
trusts in *and* relies on Me] as the Scripture has
said, From his innermost being shall flow [con-
tinuously] springs *and* rivers of living water. But
He was speaking here of the Spirit, Whom those
who believed (trusted, had faith) in Him were
afterward to receive (John 7:38–39).

No matter what is going on today, you can drink
from your own well of joy through the indwelling
presence of God's Spirit.

Enjoy Whatever You Are Doing

And there you shall eat before the Lord your God,
and you shall rejoice in all to which you put your
hand, you and your households, in which the
Lord your God has blessed you.

DEUTERONOMY 12:7

I used to hate waiting in the airport, but Dave always wanted to arrive early. I finally changed my mind. It is amazing what happens when you decide to enjoy God every day. It is easy to get so caught up in all your responsibilities that you forget to enjoy what you are doing.

You can get so busy raising your children that you forget to enjoy them. You can get so caught up in cleaning your house, trying to pay for it, and remodeling it, that you forget to enjoy it. But you can learn to enjoy God so much that no matter what you do today, you can truly say, "I enjoyed it."

Don't Worry

For You make him to be blessed and *a blessing*
forever; You make him exceedingly glad
with the joy of Your presence.

PSALM 21:6

It is a learning process to keep the devil from stealing your joy, because he constantly tempts you in new ways to lose your peace. If Satan gets your peace, then he will get your joy. Be strong and resist his temptation to make you worry.

The Word says that God gives riches and possessions, and the power to enjoy them. To accept our appointed lot and to rejoice in our work is the gift of God. We won't remember seriously the days of our life, because the tranquility of God is mirrored in us (see Ecclesiastes 5:19–20). Determine that from this day forward you will do everything you can to keep your peace and enjoy your life.

Triumph Over Troubles

Moreover [let us also be full of joy now!] let us exult and triumph in our troubles and rejoice in our sufferings, knowing that pressure and affliction and hardship produce patient and unswerving endurance.

ROMANS 5:3

Some days it seems that everything goes wrong, one thing after another, after another. Don't just talk to yourself, saying, "I just can't take anymore of this." Don't talk to your friends, saying, "I just can't put up with anymore of this."

Don't struggle with the same tests day after day; instead, talk back to the devil as Jesus did (see Luke 4:1–13). If you feel your peace and joy slipping away, talk out loud to Satan. If he is trying to steal from you, say, "Forget it, devil; you are not getting me upset today!"

Joy Makes You Strong

As for God, His way is perfect; the word of the Lord is tried. He is a Shield to all those who trust and take refuge in Him.

2 SAMUEL 22:31

Nehemiah 8:10 says, "Be not grieved *and* depressed, for the joy of the Lord is your strength *and* stronghold." Being happy and joyful makes you strong, and being mad or sad makes you weak. But the Lord is a Shield, and the Lifter of your head (see Psalm 3:3).

Satan isn't after your joy; he is after your strength. The devil wants you too weak to pray. He wants you worn out and burned out. But the Lord will lift your head and shield you from the devil's plot against you, if you put your trust in Him.

One Day at a Time

My God, my Rock, in Him will I take refuge;
my Shield and the Horn of my salvation; my
Stronghold and my Refuge, my Savior —
You save me from violence.

2 SAMUEL 22:3

Trials can come like a freight train — one car after another, after another — but eventually the last car passes. When problems seem unceasing, remind yourself, "This too shall pass." Deal with one trial at a time in the power of the Holy Ghost until each series of events is over. God will give you fresh anointing daily to handle everything that comes into your life.

Each time you endure a tough day, you can sleep it off and start again the next day. So you may as well enjoy the tough days too, because God's favor is for a lifetime; weeping may endure for a night, but joy comes in the morning (see Psalm 30:5).

Experience *His* Joy

> *Yet I will rejoice in the* LORD, *I will joy in*
> *the God of my salvation.*
>
> HABAKKUK 3:18 KJV

God created us with the ability to laugh, so we must *need* to laugh. The Word says, "A happy heart is good medicine *and* a cheerful mind works healing" (Proverbs 17:22). Jesus said that His joy would be *in* us so that we may experience His delight; He wants to fill our hearts with His gladness (see John 17:13). Jesus wants us to *experience* His joy, not just preach about it, or read books about it. He wants us to *experience* His joy.

Joy greatly depends on how you view life, so if you need help getting your sense of humor back, ask God to show you the lighter side of life today. Don't hesitate to laugh when you suddenly feel joyful; you will quickly find that joy is very contagious.

Go with the Flow

*Brethren, for this reason, in [spite of all] our stress
and crushing difficulties we have been filled with
comfort and cheer about you [because of] your faith
(the leaning of your whole personality on God in
complete trust and confidence).*

1 THESSALONIANS 3:7

Go with the flow, and stop being anxious about things that may never happen. If you really trust God, you don't need a backup plan. Faith means that you have peace even when you don't have all the answers.

Life will always be stressful if you constantly try to rearrange it. For example, getting upset in a traffic jam doesn't get you out of it any sooner. But planning for obstacles will inspire you to leave a little earlier for your appointments and keep you from hurrying. Grow in wisdom, and place high priority on keeping your peace in spite of any jams you get into today.

Enjoy Ordinary Days

They who sow in tears shall reap
in joy and singing.
PSALM 126:5

Our days in the kingdom of God are like seeds scattered upon the ground. We must continue to sleep and rise, night and day, while the seeds that we sow through our words and deeds sprout and grow and increase (see Mark 4:26–28).

Most days are not full of excitement, and some days are more difficult to endure than others. But we can learn to enjoy the ordinary and the challenging days of our lives. As the earth produces first the blade, then the ear, and finally the full grain in the ear, so will our lives produce a great harvest from our faithfulness in sowing righteousness.

Continue to do what you know is right to do, and enjoy this ordinary day. You are one day closer to a joyful harvest.

Stay Stable

The [uncompromisingly] righteous shall flourish like the palm tree [be long-lived, stately, upright, useful, and fruitful]; they shall grow like a cedar in Lebanon [majestic, stable, durable, and incorruptible].

PSALM 92:12

James 1:12 says, "Blessed (happy, to be envied) is the man who is patient under trial *and* stands up under temptation, for when he has stood the test *and* been approved, he will receive [the victor's] crown of life which God has promised to those who love Him."

Don't get upset if somebody gives you a hard time today. Don't get upset if you don't get your way, or if somebody says or does something you don't like. If you are set up for an upset, stay stable — it is only a test.

Do Your Best

But if anyone should sin, we have an Advocate
(One Who will intercede for us) with the Father —
[it is] Jesus Christ . . . And He [that same Jesus
Himself] is the propitiation (the atoning sacrifice)
for our sins, and not for ours alone but also for
[the sins of] the whole world.

1 JOHN 2:1—2

You are responsible *to* people, but God has not made you responsible *for* their joy. You may have children, or siblings, or a spouse God has given you to love and nurture who seem uninterested in your testimony. Some people just refuse to be happy, so don't let them steal your joy.

You cannot *fix* anyone, and you shouldn't take the blame for everything that goes wrong in someone else's life. Obviously, you cannot make everybody you know believe in Jesus. But you can get up every day and do your best, and then trust God for the rest.

God Is Always Working

Furthermore, brethren, we beg and admonish
you in [virtue of our union with] the Lord Jesus, that
[you follow the instructions which] you learned from
us about how you ought to walk so as to please and
gratify God, as indeed you are doing, [and] that you
do so even more and more abundantly [attaining yet
greater perfection in living this life].

1 THESSALONIANS 4:1

In 1 Thessalonians 2:13, Paul wrote, "When you received the message of God [which you heard] from us, you welcomed it not as the word of [mere] men, but as it truly is, the Word of God, *which is effectually at work in you who believe* [exercising its superhuman power *in those who adhere to and trust in and rely on it*]" (emphasis mine).

The Bible says that God's Word works in those who believe it. So no matter what you see today, believe that God is working on your breakthrough.

Look to What Is Unseen

*Clothe yourselves therefore, as God's own chosen
ones (His own picked representatives), [who are]
purified and holy and well-beloved [by God Himself,
by putting on behavior marked by] tenderhearted pity
and mercy, kind feeling, a lowly opinion of yourselves, gentle ways, [and] patience [which is tireless
and long-suffering, and has the power to endure
whatever comes, with good temper].*

COLOSSIANS 3:12

When you pray for other people, it may seem that they get worse before they get better. The devil wants to discourage you from believing that God is answering your prayers. The apostle Paul said that he learned not to be discouraged even when going through terrible trials. He said to look to the things that are unseen, not to the things that are seen (see 2 Corinthians 4:18).

Keep believing, and the power of the Holy Spirit will fill you with joy and peace until you are overflowing with hope (see Romans 15:13). Always trust God to answer your prayers.

Ignore Distractions

And when they raised their eyes,
they saw no one but Jesus only.

MATTHEW 17:8

Our own flaws can distract us from keeping our eyes on Jesus. If we think too much about what is wrong with us, we will forget what God can do through us. If we look too much at what we lack, we will forget to be thankful for what we have.

The Bible says to look away from all that will distract us from focusing on Jesus (see Hebrews 12:2). If your faith begins to waver, quickly get your eyes on Jesus, who is the Source of your faith and the Incentive for your belief. Remember how He endured the cross, despising and ignoring the shame of it, for the joy of winning you to Himself. He promises to bring your faith to maturity and perfection.

Be Thankful

*Be happy [in your faith] and rejoice and be glad-
hearted continually (always); be unceasing in prayer
[praying perseveringly]; thank [God] in everything
[no matter what the circumstances may be, be
thankful and give thanks], for this is the will of
God for you [who are] in Christ Jesus [the Revealer
and Mediator of that will]. Do not quench
(suppress or subdue) the [Holy] Spirit.*

I THESSALONIANS 5:16—19

Be thankful for everything, and be careful not to quench the Holy Spirit by complaining, or you will lose your joy. You can be gladhearted no matter what your circumstances are.

Renew your mind to God's ideals and attitude (see Romans 12:2). If you spend time in God's presence, you will think differently about yourself, and about the people around you. You will have the mind of Christ, and be full of His love.

Discipline Brings Success

But if from there you will seek (inquire for and require as necessity) the Lord your God, you will find Him if you [truly] seek Him with all your heart [and mind] and soul and life.

DEUTERONOMY 4:29

Proverbs 5:23 says that a person "will die for lack of discipline *and* instruction, and in the greatness of his folly he will go astray *and* be lost." That doesn't necessarily mean that a person will die immediately, but a lack of discipline leads toward deathly situations.

In his book *A Pursuit of God*, A. W. Tozier said (paraphrased) that God puts a desire in us to seek Him. But we have to discipline ourselves to seek Him. We can become too passive waiting for God to initiate a relationship with us. If you want to have a successful life, discipline yourself to seek God every day.

Balance Life

*Blessed (happy, fortunate, to be envied) is the man
whom You discipline and instruct, O Lord, and teach
out of Your law, that You may give him power to
keep himself calm in the days of adversity.*

PSALM 94:12—13

A person who is lazy and passive is not happy. A passive person is someone who *wants* something good to happen, but who just sits still and waits to see if it does. Successful people live disciplined lives.

First Peter 5:8 says, "Be well balanced (temperate, sober of mind), be vigilant *and* cautious at all times." The devil would like you to go overboard in some area, but stay steady and God "will Himself complete *and* make you what you ought to be, establish *and* ground you securely, and strengthen, and settle you" (v. 10).

God Works While You Rest

*Now to Him Who, by (in consequence of) the
[action of His] power that is at work within us, is
able to [carry out His purpose and] do superabundantly, far over and above all that we [dare]
ask or think [infinitely beyond our highest prayers,
desires, thoughts, hopes, or dreams].*

EPHESIANS 3:20

Being well-balanced means that you don't
do too much of one thing and not enough
of another. If you go overboard to be disciplined,
you can become legalistic, rigid, and boring! Learn
to have fun too.

Don't spend the whole day working, but don't
be lazy either. Ask God to help you balance hard
work and rest. Stop working long enough to be
thankful for all God gives you to celebrate throughout the day. As you rest in God, He will continue
working in you to help you become all He plans for
you to be.

Make Time with God a Priority

Then Jesus, knowing that they meant to come and seize Him that they might make Him king, withdrew again to the hillside by Himself alone.

JOHN 6:15

If the devil can't convince you to be idle and passive, he will drive you to do too much. As soon as you are out of balance, he can devour you (see 1 Peter 5:8). The word *disciple* comes from the word *discipline*. To be a disciple of Jesus, you must discipline yourself to follow His ways.

Jesus spent a great deal of time going about doing good for people, but He balanced His time by getting alone to pray and commune with the Father. Time with God renews your strength to do good things that you want to do for others. Live a balanced life by spending time with Him.

Walk in Love

And walk in love, [esteeming and delighting in one another] as Christ loved us and gave Himself up for us, a slain offering and sacrifice to God [for you, so that it became] a sweet fragrance.

EPHESIANS 5:2

Jesus said, "If anyone intends to come after Me, let him *deny himself [forget, ignore, disown, and lose sight of himself and his own interests]* and take up his cross, and [joining Me as a disciple and siding with My party] follow with Me [continually, cleaving steadfastly to Me] (Mark 8:34, emphasis mine).

Living a disciplined life means laying aside personal feelings, deciphering which choice is most important in God's eyes, and then allowing that choice to take preeminence over the others. As Jesus laid down His life for you, He is asking you to lay down your interests for His greater cause.

Crucify Selfish Attitudes

All of you must keep awake (give strict attention, be cautious and active) and watch and pray, that you may not come into temptation. The spirit indeed is willing, but the flesh is weak.

MATTHEW 26:41

To live in victory, we can't make decisions according to the way we feel, or by what we think we want. The Word teaches that we are born with appetites sensitive to our human nature. Our natural flesh is carnal and unspiritual. It will keep us slaves to sin, unless we crucify it and follow what the Spirit of God leads us to do.

Studying God's Word will build your faith and keep you on the right path: "The wise also will hear and increase in learning, and the person of understanding will acquire skill *and* attain to sound counsel [so that he may be able to steer his course rightly]" (Proverbs 1:5).

Choose the Narrow Path

*Enter through the narrow gate; for wide is the
gate and spacious and broad is the way that leads
away to destruction, and many are those who are
entering through it. But the gate is narrow
(contracted by pressure) and the way is straitened
and compressed that leads away to life, and
few are those who find it.*

MATTHEW 7:13–14

Even when we know the right thing to
do, it can be difficult to do if we don't *feel*
like it. We may feel like lying in bed much longer
than we should, even when we aren't sleepy anymore. Sometimes we know we ought to keep our
mouth shut, but we don't *feel* like it.

The way to victory is a narrow path that requires
discipline regardless of our feelings. Sometimes it
may look too narrow to even squeeze through. But
victory comes by obeying God's Word to us, in spite
of our feelings. Follow faith, not feelings, today.

Don't Avoid Hard Work

*For the time being no discipline brings joy, but
seems grievous and painful; but afterwards it yields a
peaceable fruit of righteousness to those who have
been trained by it [a harvest of fruit which consists in
righteousness — in conformity to God's will in
purpose, thought, and action, resulting in right
living and right standing with God].*

HEBREWS 12:11

An undisciplined person looks for ways to avoid hard work. Passivity prevails in our culture; everything is geared toward making life easier: ride the escalator, take the elevator, get fast-food carryout. But the easy way is not always the best way.

Just as we need to exercise our bodies, so we also need to exercise our faith by facing difficult challenges. Use faith to forgive those who offend you and to trust God when you can't see how problems will be solved. Soon you will enjoy a harvest of righteousness from the discipline you endure today.

Make the Most of Time

*Where is the wise man (the philosopher)? Where is
the scribe (the scholar)? Where is the investigator (the
logician, the debater) of this present time and age?
Has not God shown up the nonsense and the
folly of this world's wisdom?*

I CORINTHIANS 1:20

In Ephesians 5:15–17 God's Word says
that we are to live purposefully, using
wisdom as sensible, intelligent people. This means
to make the most of the time we are given. Equal
time is given to us all, but we don't always use wisdom to keep from wasting it.

We are to buy up every opportunity we can to
fulfill our purpose on earth, which is to love God and
others. Verse 17 says, "Therefore do not be vague
and thoughtless *and* foolish, but understanding *and*
firmly grasping what the will of the Lord is." Get
alone with God to make sure you know how to use
your time today.

Words Are Power

Exercise foresight and *be on the watch to look [after one another], to see that no one falls back from and fails to secure God's grace (His unmerited favor and spiritual blessing), in order that no root of resentment (rancor, bitterness, or hatred) shoots forth and causes trouble* and *bitter torment, and the many become contaminated* and *defiled by it.*

HEBREWS 12:15

Jesus said, "If you have faith (a firm relying trust) and do not doubt . . . even if you *say* to this mountain, Be taken up and cast into the sea, it will be done. And *whatever you ask* for in prayer, having faith *and* [really] believing, you will receive" (Matthew 21:21–22, emphasis mine).

Don't misuse the power of words by *talking too much* without faith or *talking too little* about your faith. Choose kind and gentle words that lift people and quiet gossip and strife. Believe that God's grace will prevail through what you say.

Balance Discipline

And I will walk at liberty and at ease, for I have
sought and inquired for [and desperately
required] Your precepts.

PSALM 119:45

It takes discipline to balance your life. You should be disciplined to pray, disciplined to read and study the Word, and disciplined to spend quality time in fellowship with the Lord. But you must also be disciplined to spend quality time with your family, and to take care of your health. You should even discipline yourself to rest and have fun.

Examine your life today, and do what is needed to bring balance to the way you use your time. God wants your life to be full of joy. Psalm 23:2–3 teaches that He will lead you beside still and restful waters. He will refresh and restore your life. And He will lead you in the paths of righteousness for His name's sake.

Write the Vision

Where there is no vision [no redemptive revelation
of God], the people perish; but he who keeps the law
[of God, which includes that of man] — blessed
(happy, fortunate, and enviable) is he.

The Lord told Habakkuk to write the vision that God had given him, and to engrave it so plainly on tablets that everyone who passed could read it easily. God promised that His vision would be fulfilled on its appointed day (see Habakkuk 2:2–3).

If you have been asking God to lead you in the way you should go, you will have a sense of purpose building in you. You can ask Him to help you plan your day, your week, and your life. I encourage you to write down the things that God imprints on your heart to do. Writing the vision, and placing it where you can routinely see it, will help settle the plan God puts inside of you.

Live with Purpose

Therefore, my beloved brethren, be firm (steadfast),
immovable, always abounding in the work of the Lord
[always being superior, excelling, doing more than
enough in the service of the Lord], knowing and being
continually aware that your labor in the Lord is not
futile [it is never wasted or to no purpose].

1 CORINTHIANS 15:58

Life without purpose is vanity. Webster's definition of *purpose* is "something set up as an object or end to be attained." Christians ought to be people with purpose. We are all purposed to seek the kingdom of God, which is His righteousness, peace, and joy in the Holy Spirit (see Romans 14:17).

Today is an opportunity to willfully and deliberately seek God with the intent to know Him better than we knew Him yesterday. Today we can deliberately move forward with the intent to accomplish good things for the kingdom.

Stay on Course

*Let your eyes look right on [with fixed purpose],
and let your gaze be straight before you. Consider well
the path of your feet, and let all your ways be established and ordered aright. Turn not aside to the right
hand or to the left; remove your foot from evil.*

PROVERBS 4:25–27

Jesus knew what His purpose was. He disciplined Himself to stay on course, living His life to fulfill that purpose for which He came. As Christians, we need to follow in His steps and focus on our purpose. We were bought with a price to live our lives in such a way that we become the salt of the earth, the light of the world (see Matthew 5).

We are to lay down our selfish, self-centered life-styles, and gear our lives toward doing something for the betterment of someone else. Then we will experience that "joy unspeakable, and full of glory" (1 Peter 1:8).

Keep Alert

Blessed (happy, fortunate, and to be envied) are
those servants whom the master finds awake and alert
and watching when he comes. Truly I say to you, he
will gird himself and have them recline at table and
will come and serve them!

LUKE 12:37

In Ephesians 6:10 God's word teaches, "Be strong in the Lord [be empowered through your union with Him]; draw your strength from Him [that strength which His boundless might provides]." We are to put on God's armor so we won't be deceived by the devil. Verse 16 says, "Lift up over all the [covering] shield of saving faith, upon which you can quench all the flaming missiles of the wicked [one]."

In verse 18 we are also told to "pray at all times (on every occasion, in every season) in the Spirit, with all [manner of] prayer and entreaty. *To that end keep alert and watch with strong purpose and perseverance,* interceding in behalf of all the saints (God's consecrated people)" (emphasis mine).

Act Now

The Spirit of the Lord [is] upon Me, because He
has anointed Me [the Anointed One, the Messiah] to
preach the good news (the Gospel) to the poor;
He has sent Me to announce release to the captives
and recovery of sight to the blind, to send forth as
delivered those who are oppressed [who are downtrod-
den, bruised, crushed, and broken down by calamity].

LUKE 4:18

Good intentions are not acts of obedience, and procrastination devours opportunities to live a purposeful life. Whatever God
has inspired you to do — do it today.

Just do what needs to be done, even if the first
thing you tackle is the dishes in the kitchen sink or a
garage that needs cleaning. If God has specifically
told you to bless someone, and you have intended to
do it, remember that *now* is the acceptable time, *now*
is the day of salvation (see 2 Corinthians 6:2).

Win the Race

But [like a boxer] I buffet my body [handle it roughly, discipline it by hardships] and subdue it, for fear that after proclaiming to others the Gospel and things pertaining to it, I myself should become unfit [not stand the test, be unapproved and rejected as a counterfeit].

1 CORINTHIANS 9:27

It is easy to leave unpleasant tasks for later. But God wants His people to finish the race that He sets before them to run (see 2 Timothy 4:7). Don't be afraid to do what seems to be hard. God will anoint you to do whatever He tells you to do.

Paul spoke of this race for the sake of the gospel in 1 Corinthians 9:23–26: "So run [your race] that you may lay hold [of the prize] *and* make it yours." He said to run with definite aim, and to discipline yourself to finish the race. Grace will make winning easier than you imagined.

Brace Your Mind

I am able to do nothing from Myself [indepen-
dently, of My own accord — but only as I am taught
by God and as I get His orders].

JOHN 5:30

One of the reasons people don't get things done is that they mentally see their unfinished assignments as monstrous undertakings. If they would just take care of those projects, they would find they aren't that big of a deal.

First Peter 1:13 says, "Brace up your minds; be sober (circumspect, morally alert); set your hope wholly *and* unchangeably on the grace (divine favor) that is coming to you when Jesus Christ (the Messiah) is revealed." Don't let your mind rule you. When thoughts of inadequacy fill your head, stop and remember that God's grace is sufficient to meet all your needs. Just do things one at a time, and keep your mind on God's ability, not your own.

Keep a Positive Attitude

*Keep your foot [give your mind to what
you are doing] when you go [as Jacob to sacred
Bethel] to the house of God. For to draw near to
hear and obey is better than to give the sacrifice of
fools [carelessly, irreverently] too ignorant to
know that they are doing evil.*

ECCLESIASTES 5:1

People who take a positive attitude and say, "I can do it. I am going to do it right now. It is no problem. Everything will work out fine," are wonderful to be around and work with because they tackle things and get them done.

If you put off something you should have done already, it will start to threaten you with fear. Don't allow an assignment to get out of proportion in your mind. Keep your mind on what you set out to do today. If you get interrupted, make yourself come back to that task and finish it up. Nothing is so hard that you can't handle it, if you will keep a positive attitude and do it God's way.

Have a Plan

Make me go in the path of Your commandments,
for in them do I delight.

PSALM 119:35

Go to sleep at night with a plan in mind for the next day. Don't be vague about what you hope to accomplish. One morning I was lying in bed when the Spirit of the Lord said to me, "Stop being ambiguous." The dictionary defines *ambiguous* as "doubtful or uncertain," and "capable of being understood in two or more possible senses or ways."

Don't be double-minded. Don't just wait to see what happens. Wake up with a plan that puts God first in all you do. God's Word is a lamp to your feet, and a light to your path (see Psalm 119:105). Talk to Him before you even get out of bed; ask Him to make clear what you need to achieve today.

Develop Self-control

He who has no rule over his own spirit is like a
city that is broken down and without walls.

PROVERBS 25:28

Self-control is a fruit of the Spirit (see Galatians 5:22–23). It develops as we spend time fellowshipping with God and practicing obedience to Him. Sometimes we would rather that God control us and make us do the right thing. But He wants us to rule over our spirit.

Proverbs 16:32 says, "He who is slow to anger is better than the mighty, he who rules his [own] spirit than he who takes a city." It takes self-control not to get offended, not to become angry every time somebody doesn't do something the way we want it done. Self-control is needed over our thoughts, our words, and our appetites. But once we master our own spirit, we are considered to be powerful in the eyes of God — stronger than one who takes a city.

Don't Be Lazy

Do you see a man diligent and skillful in his business? He will stand before kings; he will not stand before obscure men.

PROVERBS 22:29

Proverbs 24:30–34 gives a clear warning about being lazy. Laziness allows everything in our lives to get overgrown or broken down. We are to observe the fate of a lazy man and receive this instruction: "Yet a little sleep, a little slumber, a little folding of the hands to sleep — so shall your poverty come as a robber."

God will help you with anything in your life that has become overgrown or broken down. If you put your trust in Him, He can turn your mess into your message. Set your way to follow God from this day forth. Guard against the spirit of laziness. Get rid of procrastination, and do whatever God has been telling you to do.

Appreciate Correction

Happy (blessed, fortunate, enviable) is the man who finds skillful and godly Wisdom, and the man who gets understanding [drawing it forth from God's Word and life's experiences], for the gaining of it is better than the gaining of silver, and the profit of it better than fine gold.

PROVERBS 3:13–14

Ask God to reveal areas in which you need to apply self-control. You can even enjoy the journey to becoming all that He has in mind for you to be, if you learn to appreciate godly correction from others. Remember, God loves you just the way you are, but He corrects those He loves (see Proverbs 3:12).

Only mature Christians enjoy the meat of God's Word, and He has much to share with His grown-up sons and daughters. There will always be more to learn, so don't make excuses for your weak points. Accepting the truth will set you free (see John 8:32), and God will give you strength to overcome in those areas in which you are weak.

Fruit of the Spirit

If we live by the [Holy] Spirit, let us also walk
by the Spirit. [If by the Holy Spirit we have our
life in God, let us go forward walking in line,
our conduct controlled by the Spirit.]

GALATIANS 5:25

People crave love, happiness, and peace. They try to buy these things and pay therapists to help them find them. All these qualities are available by trusting as their Savior, Jesus, who sends the Holy Spirit to help them walk in obedience to God. Living the Spirit-filled life will eventually produce those things that people want most in their lives.

Galatians 5:22–23 says, "But the fruit of the [Holy] Spirit [the work which His presence within accomplishes] is love, joy (gladness), peace, patience (an even temper, forbearance), kindness, goodness (benevolence), faithfulness, gentleness (meekness, humility), self-control (self-restraint, continence). Against such things there is no law [that can bring a charge]." Let the work of God's presence within you shine through you to others today.

Be Diligent

*But we do [strongly and earnestly] desire for
each of you to show the same diligence and sincerity
[all the way through] in realizing and enjoying
the full assurance and development of [your]
hope until the end.*

HEBREWS 6:11

Proverbs 22:29 says, "Do you see a man diligent *and* skillful in his business? He will stand before kings; he will not stand before obscure men." A diligent man lives by the principle of "just do it!" He is the one who does it, does it, does it, and then does it some more, until whatever he set out to do is finished.

Never give up on anything God has told you to believe for; never quit doing anything He has clearly shown you to do. Your diligence will pay off with a blessing from God.

Complete Your Work

Jesus said to them, My food (nourishment) is to do the will (pleasure) of Him Who sent Me and to accomplish and completely finish His work.

JOHN 4:34

I believe the Lord wants us to finish whatever He calls us to do, even when it requires patience, perseverance, and hard work. God wants us to grow roots and learn to endure until the fruit of His promise is manifested.

Be willing to endure patiently to see God's plan take place in your life. If God has given you a vision of something He wants you to accomplish, keep doing whatever He has given you to do, even when the excitement for the work is over, and all the goose bumps are gone. If you don't have a vision, ask God to show you something that you need to do, and then commit your work to the Lord until it is completed.

Rid Yourself of Clutter

"You will keep him *in perfect peace,* whose *mind is stayed* on You, *because he trusts in You."*

ISAIAH 26:3 NKJ

Sometimes we complicate our life by taking on things that God has not told us to do. We add stress, confusion, and clutter with the unnecessary things we take on and hold on to. We need to use our faith to let go of whatever clutters our mind and keeps us from peace.

Ask God to show you ways to simplify your life. Take an inventory today, and start throwing out whatever is filling your life with unproductive distractions. God wants you to enjoy your day, so get rid of whatever He shows you to give up.

Love Your Critics

*He who heeds instruction and correction is
[not only himself] in the way of life [but also]
is a way of life for others.*

PROVERBS 10:17

Love your critics. Appreciate people's correction. Appreciate God's correction also. Proverbs 3:12 says, "For whom the Lord loves He corrects."

Self-discipline is the mark of maturity. If you don't have control of yourself in a certain area, you are undisciplined. In that area you are not mature. If you want to be a mature Christian, then you must be disciplined.

If you want to be free to truly enjoy your life, you must face the truth. You cannot be free if you make excuses for any area of weakness that God has pointed out to you. Everyone has weaknesses: give thanks to God if you discover one of yours today, and trust Him to be strong in that area in your behalf.

Get Rid of Hindrances

Purge (clean out) the old leaven that you may
be fresh (new) dough, still uncontaminated
[as you are], for Christ.

1 CORINTHIANS 5:7

If you are serious about growing in the Lord and reaching a maturity of faith, you will embrace Matthew 5:29–30. It is a powerful Scripture which basically says: "If your eye offends you, pluck it out; if your hand offends you, cut it off."

In 1 Corinthians 9:24–27, Paul said, "I am running a race, and *I am running it to win*. Therefore, I buffet my body, I subdue it, and I handle it roughly" (paraphrased).

If you have habits or hindrances in your life that are fouling you up, get rid of them. Do it *now!* Don't waste today with regret. Ask God to show you any area in your life that needs discipline, and then draw from His vast supply of grace to make the changes you need to make.

Control Your Moods

Receive instruction in wise dealing and *the discipline of wise thoughtfulness, righteousness, justice, and integrity.*

PROVERBS 1:3

Moods can bring strange impulses that we dare not heed. When we get moody, we want to do weird things, or neglect our responsibilities.

"I don't feel like doing anything today. I am in a bad mood. Just leave me alone."

Disciplined people submit their emotions to wisdom. They say, "These are my feelings, but I don't live by my feelings. I may have moods, but they don't dictate my actions. I am going to do exactly what I would do if I felt better." You will enjoy your day more when you discipline yourself to do what you believe, instead of what you feel.

Control Your Speech

A gentle tongue [with its healing
power] is a tree of life.

PROVERBS 15:4

The Bible says that if a person can control his speech, he can curb his entire nature: "For we all often stumble *and* fall *and* offend in many things. And if anyone does not offend in speech [never says the wrong things], he is a fully developed character *and* a perfect man, able to control his whole body *and* to curb his entire nature"(James 3:2).

No one is completely mature in the Lord, so there is always room for improvement. If your mouth is out of control, other areas of your life will also be out of control. Give your speech to God today. Ask Him to direct the words you speak, and allow Him to fill your mouth with words of life that lift up everyone around you.

Choose Excellence

I am Your servant; give me understanding
(discernment and comprehension), that I may know
(discern and be familiar with the character of)
Your testimonies.

PSALM 119:125

The Word says, "Learn to sense what is vital, *and* approve *and* prize what is excellent *and* of real value [recognizing the highest and the best, and distinguishing the moral differences], and . . . be untainted *and* pure and unerring *and* blameless [so that with hearts sincere and certain and unsullied, you may approach] the day of Christ [not stumbling *nor* causing others to stumble]" (Philippians 1:10).

People make choices and selections all day long. A truly disciplined person has the ability to subordinate the lesser choice to the greater, more excellent choice. Think about that as you choose the way you will go today. Select the greater cause, and subordinate the lesser options to it.

You Are Secure

Lean on, trust in, and *be confident in the Lord with all your heart* and *mind and do not rely on your own insight* or *understanding. In all your ways know, recognize,* and *acknowledge Him, and He will direct* and *make straight* and *plain your paths.*

Following God is not a part-time lifestyle. The Bible clearly teaches that we are to be cautious *at all times* because the devil looks for opportunities to devour us (see 1 Peter 5:8).

But God gives us grace to withstand the devil and to be firm in faith against his onset. You can be rooted, established strong, immovable, and determined, knowing that whatever you face today is identical to what Christians throughout the world are facing. And God Himself will complete you and make you what you ought to be. He will establish you and ground you securely, strengthen and settle you today (see vv. 9—10).

Use Self-Control

*For this very reason, make every effort to add
to your faith goodness; and to goodness, knowledge;
and to knowledge, self-control; and to self-control,
perseverance; and to perseverance, godliness; and
to godliness, brotherly kindness; and to brotherly
kindness, love. For if you possess these qualities in
increasing measure, they will keep you from being
ineffective and unproductive in your knowledge
of our Lord Jesus Christ.*

2 PETER 1:5–8 NIV

The Word says that a person will die for lack of discipline and instruction, and in his folly he will go astray and be lost (see Proverbs 5:23). You can't buy discipline, but you have an inner ability to develop self-control.

By spending time with God, you can be filled with His Spirit and controlled by His power to live a calm life with a well-balanced mind of discipline and self-control (see 2 Timothy 1:7). Consciously add self-control to your behavior today.

Give God Control

*And endurance (fortitude) develops maturity of
character (approved faith and tried integrity). And
character [of this sort] produces [the habit of]
joyful and confident hope of eternal salvation.*

ROMANS 5:4

You will not enjoy your day if anything is
out of control. You can keep your temper,
moods, emotions, appetite, mouth, and thoughts in
line with God's Word if you give Him control over
the areas you want to subdue with faith. God created
us with a free will, and we can choose the thing that
is best for us.

Be free from old destructive habits by simply
forming new ones. Don't let your emotions get out
of control today. If, for instance, you feel your temper begin to rise, pray quickly for God to fill you
with the fruit of the Spirit. Use the self-control that
He freely makes available to you.

Desire God's Heart

Arm yourselves with the same thought and purpose [patiently to suffer rather than fail to please God]. For whoever has suffered in the flesh [having the mind of Christ] is done with [intentional] sin [has stopped pleasing himself and the world, and pleases God], so that he can no longer spend the rest of his natural life living by [his] human appetites and desires, but [he lives] for what God wills.

1 PETER 4:1—2

You have desires of the flesh, but you also have desires inspired by the Holy Spirit. You have a mind of flesh, but you also "have the mind of Christ" and "hold the thoughts (feelings and purposes) of His heart" (1 Corinthians 2:16).

Learn to determine where your desires are coming from. Desires from your flesh don't bring peace, but desires from God's Spirit bring joyful rewards. Exercise self-control, and choose those desires that are planted in you by the Holy Spirit.

Don't Waste Time

Look carefully then how you walk! Live pur-posefully and worthily and accurately, not as the unwise and witless, but as wise (sensible, intelligent people), making the very most of the time [buying up each opportunity].

EPHESIANS 5:15–16

We need to be so self-controlled that we don't waste time. That doesn't mean that we can never do anything fun. It doesn't mean we can't do things that we enjoy.

We don't need to be rigid, stiff, or boring. But we do need to use our time wisely, choosing to give the best part of our day to spend time with God.

The Word encourages us to be prepared, saying, "Hear counsel, receive instruction, *and* accept cor-rection, that you may be wise in the time to come" (Proverbs 19:20). Starting your day with God's in-struction will keep you walking in wisdom, making the most of your time.

Initiate Solutions

I have set before you life and death, the blessings
and the curses; therefore choose life.

DEUTERONOMY 30:19

Sometimes we complain about things that we could change if we would stop feeling sorry for ourselves long enough to do something about them. For example, if we are lonely, we can make the effort to be a friend to someone else. We can choose to be free or remain in bondage to self-pity. We can choose to be pitiful or powerful.

Psalm 25:12–14 says, "Who is the man who reverently fears *and* worships the Lord? Him shall He teach in the way that he should choose. He himself shall dwell at ease, and his offspring shall inherit the land. The secret [of the sweet, satisfying companionship] of the Lord have they who fear (revere and worship) Him, and He will show them His covenant *and* reveal to them its [deep, inner] meaning."

Admirable Virtues

But I say, walk and live [habitually] in the
[Holy] Spirit [responsive to and controlled and
guided by the Spirit]; then you will certainly not
gratify the cravings and desires of the flesh
(of human nature without God).

GALATIANS 5:16

"The fruit of the [Holy] Spirit, [the work which His presence within accomplishes] is love, joy (gladness), peace, patience (an even temper, forbearance), kindness, goodness (benevolence), faithfulness, gentleness (meekness, humility), self-control (self-restraint, continence)" (Galatians 5:22–23).

People throughout the world try to acquire these virtues through counseling or self-help books. Yet the Bible says that if we walk with God, the Spirit-filled life will produce all these things within us. Give your life to God each day, and He will create a right heart in you, one that will want to do the things He would have you do.

Sowing and Reaping

So then, as occasion and opportunity open up to us, let us do good [morally] to all people [not only being useful or profitable to them, but also doing what is for their spiritual good and advantage]. Be mindful to be a blessing, especially to those of the household of faith [those who belong to God's family with you, the believers].

GALATIANS 6:10

"For he who sows to his own flesh (lower nature, sensuality) will from the flesh reap decay *and* ruin *and* destruction, but he who sows to the Spirit will from the Spirit reap eternal life" (Galatians 6:8).

We can enjoy our life (and avoid trouble) if we follow the Holy Spirit's leading. The Word tells us not to grow weary from doing what is right, because God promises that whatever we sow today we will also reap sometime in the future (see v. 9). Be courageous, act nobly, and continue doing what you know is right.

A New Direction

O Lord, You have heard the desire and *the long-ing of the humble* and *oppressed; You will prepare* and *strengthen* and *direct their hearts.*

PSALM 10:17

Sometimes we come to an unhappy place in our lives. If we examine ourselves on those days, we will most likely discover that the things that make us most unhappy are the fruit of the choices that we made earlier.

Today can be a new start. I think God gave us twenty-four-hour days because He knew that was all we could handle. His mercies are new every morning (see Lamentations 3:22–23). You can start over this morning and live today for the Lord. Determine to follow wherever God leads you, and do whatever He tells you to do. You can expect better tomorrows when you live right today.

Walk in Integrity

The Lord rewarded me according to my righteousness (my conscious integrity and sincerity with Him); according to the cleanness of my hands has He recompensed me.

PSALM 18:20

Talking about the Word isn't enough; we need to do what we say we believe. God will bless us if we are people of integrity. As believers, we need to keep our promises and do what we say we will do.

Look for ways to demonstrate integrity today. If you can't follow through with something you said you would do for someone, at least call or write a letter, saying, "Please forgive me; I was not being led by God, and I just cannot do what I said." This way you will honor God and keep your steps going in the right direction.

Stay Out of Strife

He who is of a greedy spirit stirs up strife,
but he who puts his trust in the Lord
shall be enriched and blessed.

PROVERBS 28:25

Probably 80 percent of the places we visit in our ministry have church members who are riddled with strife. Strife is the devil's tool against us. It takes personal self-control to stay out of strife.

If you want to keep peace, you can't always say everything you want to say. Sometimes you have to control yourself and apologize even when there is nothing in you that wants to do so. But if you sow the godly principle of harmony and unity today, a time will come when you will reap the blessings of all it can bring to you.

Keep Your Promises

*He who honors those who fear the Lord (who revere
and worship Him); who swears to his own hurt and
does not change; [he who] does not put out his
money for interest [to one of his own people] and
who will not take a bribe against the innocent. He
who does these things shall never be moved.*

PSALM 15:4—5

There are times when I make a commitment to do something that later I regret.
Then I try to figure out some way to get out of doing what I said I would do. I argue, "God, surely You
don't want me to do this thing and miss this other
great opportunity."

The only thing the Lord ever says to me is, "You
gave your word, Joyce. Be a woman of integrity, and
I will bless you." If we are people of integrity, God
will bring other good opportunities around another
time with even more blessings.

Ask for Help

Confess to one another therefore your faults
(your slips, your false steps, your offenses, your sins)
and pray [also] for one another, that you may be
healed and restored [to a spiritual tone of mind and
heart]. The earnest (heartfelt, continued) prayer of a
righteous man makes tremendous power available
[dynamic in its working].

JAMES 5:16

Addictions, habits, or negative attitudes can wear you out. If you need deliverance from some wrong behavior, the Bible teaches that the Holy Spirit is your Helper (see John 14:16). Confess your need to God, and ask Him to deliver you.

He may lead you to confess your faults to other believers whom you can trust to pray for you. The Word says that we are to confess our faults to one another *so that we may be healed and restored*. If you are out of control in some area, be honest about it. Today can be your day of deliverance.

Eliminate Excuses

*For the Lord your God walks in the midst of
your camp to deliver you and to give up your enemies
before you. Therefore shall your camp be holy,
that He may see nothing indecent among
you and turn away from you.*

DEUTERONOMY 23:14

If a habit is controlling you, you will not enjoy the best that God offers you. Don't make excuses for bondages that seem to have a hold on you. Denial and excuses will keep you from enjoying your life.

Whether it is an eating disorder or a bad temper, you cannot blame it on your genes or your family. God makes a way of escape for us and promises a good life for those who are born again. Claim your rights as a child of God. Say, "I am a new person in Christ; I can do all things through Christ who strengthens me" (see Philippians 4:13).

God Will Change You

Many plans are in a man's mind, but it is the
Lord's purpose for him that will stand.

PROVERBS 19:21

Even though you may still be operating in old habits, you still have hope of change, but you can't change yourself. God will change you, if you seek Him with your whole heart.

Don't be in a hurry for God to finish working in your life. We want everything to be done instantly, but God is not interested in our schedule. The enemy may thwart *your* plans, but *God's* plans don't get thwarted, and He has a unique plan for you.

Seek God's plan for your life. Stay on fire, red hot, zealous. Pursue His purpose for you with every ounce of energy you have. There is nothing in this world that is worth seeking more.

Seek God Wholeheartedly

*Seek, inquire of and for the Lord, and crave Him
and His strength (His might and inflexibility
to temptation); seek and require His face and His
presence [continually] evermore.*

PSALM 105:4

If you have a need today, seek God with your whole heart. The Bible says to "aim at *and* seek the [rich, eternal treasures] that are above" (Colossians 3:1). If you seek the fruit of the Spirit wholeheartedly, God will do a work in your life so that you will enjoy the abundant life Jesus died to give you.

God promises, "And the Lord shall make you the head, and not the tail; and you shall be above only, and you shall not be beneath, if you heed the commandments of the Lord your God which I command you this day and are watchful to do them" (Deuteronomy 28:13).

Be Positive

*I thank my God at all times for you because of
the grace (the favor and spiritual blessing) of God
which was bestowed on you in Christ Jesus, [so] that
in Him in every respect you were enriched, in full
power and readiness of speech [to speak of your
faith] and complete knowledge and illumination
[to give you full insight into its meaning].*

1 CORINTHIANS 1:4–5

The Word of God says, "Depart from evil
and do good; seek, inquire for, *and* crave
peace and pursue (go after) it!" (Psalm 34:14). "Do
all things without grumbling *and* faultfinding *and*
complaining [against God] and questioning *and*
doubting [among yourselves]" (Philippians 2:14).

Be positive. Get rid of gossiping and complaining. Start your day by reading the Bible so that you
will know how to speak from the authority of God's
Word. Spend time listening to God, and then tell
others what you hear Him say. Bring life to whatever
situations you face.

Control Your Temper

He who is slow to anger has great understanding.

PROVERBS 14:29

It is uncomfortable for others to be around us if we are easily angered. We need to learn how to *respond* to life instead of *react* to it, so that we can enjoy God's power in our lives. God says that a person who can control his or her anger is better and mightier than an individual who can take a whole city (see Proverbs 16:32).

God's Word says, "Understand [this], my beloved brethren. Let every man be quick to hear [a ready listener], slow to speak, slow to take offense *and* to get angry. For man's anger does not promote the righteousness God [wishes and requires]" (James 1:19–20). Be a ready listener, and enjoy the freedom from anger that God offers you.

Be Slow to Speak

For let him who wants to enjoy life and see good days [good — whether apparent or not] keep his tongue free from evil and his lips from guile (treachery, deceit).

1 PETER 3:10

Have you ever regretted something you said as soon as the words were out of your mouth? You can't take back the words you speak to others — and words can damage relationships. The Bible says that if you can control your mouth, you can control your whole body (see James 3:2).

Before you respond to people too quickly, stop and listen to what the Holy Spirit has to say about your situation. James taught, "Let every man be quick to hear [a ready listener], slow to speak, slow to take offense *and* to get angry" (James 1:19). Commit your mouth to God's service today, and use words that speak healing to others.

Love Isn't Touchy

Love (God's love in us) does not insist on its own rights or its own way, for it is not self-seeking; it is not touchy or fretful or resentful; it takes no account of the evil done to it [it pays no attention to a suffered wrong].

1 CORINTHIANS 13:5

The Bible says that God's love in us is not touchy. If we wear our emotions on our sleeve all the time, we may need to spend more time in His presence before we face the day. Our tears can provoke sympathy, but it is better to be a giver instead of a taker all the time.

Starting your day with God will keep you "sweetened up" and full of confidence. As you enjoy His gentleness and kindness, you will be built up in your spirit and better able to overlook the offenses of others. Ask God to give you a strong heart, one ready to love people today as He does.

Get in Balance

Love bears up under anything and *everything that comes, is ever ready to believe the best of every person, its hopes are fadeless under all circumstances, and it endures everything [without weakening].*

1 CORINTHIANS 13:7

We all get emotional occasionally or lose our temper once in a while. But if you are out of balance in either one of these areas, it is very important to get back in balance if you want your day to go right.

If your feelings get hurt because someone looks at you crossways or because friends or family forget your birthday, you need to spend more time with God. He will fill you with so much love and such a sense of self-worth that you won't feel ill-tempered or touchy toward anyone. Seek God with your whole heart today. Talk to Him about your problems, and then enjoy yourself, knowing that He cares for you.

Don't Procrastinate

*But the fruit of the [Holy] Spirit [the work
which His presence within accomplishes] is love, joy
(gladness), peace, patience (an even temper, forbearance), kindness, goodness (benevolence), faithfulness,
gentleness (meekness, humility), self-control
(self-restraint, continence). Against such things
there is no law [that can bring a charge].*

GALATIANS 5:22—23

The Bible says that we are to "be doers of
the Word [obey the message], and not
merely listeners to it" (James 1:22). In other words,
we are to apply its teaching to our everyday lives.

Procrastination is one of the greatest barriers to
putting God's word into action in our lives. It takes
self-control to *do* something, and it also takes self-
control *not* to do something. Self-control is a fruit of
the Spirit that comes into our lives by spending time
with God. Ask God to fill you with the power of
self-control in order to overcome procrastination
and be a doer of the Word.

Break Strongholds

For the weapons of our warfare are not physical
[weapons of flesh and blood], but they are mighty
before God for the overthrow and destruction of
strongholds, . . . and we lead every thought and
purpose away captive into the obedience of Christ
(the Messiah, the Anointed One).

2 CORINTHIANS 10:4–5

The Bible teaches that Satan tries to build strongholds in our lives. One way to identify the strongholds in your life is to watch for repetitive situations that pull you down in spirit.

We all know inside when something is not right in our life or is getting out of control. If that happens to you, seek God early to find out what is going on. If a negative behavior becomes repetitive, that is a signal that Satan is building himself a stronghold in your life. God will destroy the devil's strongholds within you, if you draw near to Him.

Find Truth

And you will know the Truth, and
the Truth will set you free.

JOHN 8:32

If you lose your temper easily, you will never enjoy your day as God meant for it to be. Seek God with your whole heart and find out what is wrong. The way to get free from things that upset you is to find truth — the truth will always set you free.

We don't always want to face truth because sometimes it is painful. Sometimes it shows us that we need to change. If we are behaving badly, we make excuses for our wrong behavior. But excuses will never make us free. Let God get involved with your day; when you feel your temper flare, ask Him to reveal the truth of that situation. The truth will always set you free to enjoy the rest of your day.

Get Free

Out of my distress I called upon the Lord;
the Lord answered me and set me free.

PSALM 118:5

If you find yourself running late everywhere you go (even 50 percent of the time), that is evidence of a stronghold that Satan has built in your life. Get free from it, or the devil will use it to keep you under pressure. You may have an excuse for every time you are behind schedule, but something is wrong if that behavior pattern is repetitive.

Ask God to show you how to get free from the pressure of always hurrying and being late. Starting your day with God will help you set priorities for your day. Get to the root of the problem, and enjoy the fruit of God's indwelling presence to get you where you need to be — on time and without hurrying.

Run the Race

I press on toward the goal to win the
[supreme and heavenly] prize to which God in
Christ Jesus is calling us upward.

PHILIPPIANS 3:14

We live in a society that is used to doing whatever feels good *right now*. But instant gratification never brings lasting satisfaction.

If you operate in self-control through the power of the Holy Spirit living in you, you will choose to do things that contribute to the goal that you have in mind. You must discipline yourself now so you will reap the reward of reaching your goal later.

Paul taught, "Do you not know that in a race all the runners compete, but [only] one receives the prize? So run [your race] that you may lay hold [of the prize] *and* make it yours" (1 Corinthians 9:24). Stay focused on the goal. God will give you the grace to continue moving toward it.

Get Fit

*For God did not give us a spirit of timidity
(of cowardice, of craven and cringing and fawning
fear), but [He has given us a spirit] of power and
of love and of calm and well-balanced mind
and discipline and self-control.*

2 TIMOTHY 1:7

"Every athlete who goes into training conducts himself temperately *and* restricts himself in *all* things" (1 Corinthians 9:25, emphasis mine). That word *all* is a difficult concept for us to grasp.

We need to live a disciplined life, physically, spiritually, and emotionally, if we want to enjoy God's plan for us. The fruit of the Spirit is self-control, and the fruit of the flesh is no control.

Paul said, "I buffet my body [handle it roughly, discipline it by hardships] and subdue it, for fear that after proclaiming to others the Gospel *and* things pertaining to it, I myself should become unfit [not stand the test, be unapproved and rejected as a counterfeit]" (1 Corinthians 9:27).

Be a Doer of the Word

My life makes its boast in the Lord.

PSALM 34:2

I have found three principles to be life-changing when followed faithfully every day:

1. Eliminate excuses and avoid procrastination. Being a doer of the Word is putting your faith into action. Faith without action is dead faith (see James 2:20 KJV).

2. Face the truth no matter how painful it is. Truth is the only thing that will set you free (see John 8:32). God's Word is full of truth. Start your day in the Word of God.

3. Stop feeling sorry for yourself. Understand who you are in Jesus Christ. You are more than capable in Him (see Philippians 4:13).

Enjoy the Power to Love Others

So speak and so act as [people should] who are to be judged under the law of liberty [the moral instruction given by Christ, especially about love].

JAMES 2:12

It can be difficult to grasp the idea of the "law of liberty," because law and liberty seem to be worlds apart: A law says one thing, while liberty says another. I believe the law of liberty spoken of in James 1:25 refers to the freedom of self-control, because God puts a new heart in us that *wants* to obey His law of love.

With this new heart that Jesus gave you, you have the ability to be led of the Spirit, who gives you the power and freedom to love others. Enjoy your day by allowing the Lord to love others through you.

Be Responsible

But you are not living the life of the flesh, you are living the life of the Spirit, if the [Holy] Spirit of God [really] dwells within you [directs and controls you]. But if anyone does not possess the [Holy] Spirit of Christ, he is none of His [he does not belong to Christ, is not truly a child of God].

ROMANS 8:9

Romans 8:8 declares: "Those who are living the life of the flesh [catering to the appetites and impulses of their carnal nature] cannot please *or* satisfy God, *or* be acceptable to Him."

God wants us to enjoy the good life. Here He is saying to us, "If you walk in the Spirit, you will reap blessings from the Spirit-controlled life both now and hereafter."

Be responsible for your choices today. You cannot choose to live in the flesh and still expect everything to work out well. Choose to be obedient to the leading of the Holy Spirit.

Sow What You Want to Reap

Sow for yourselves according to righteousness (uprightness and right standing with God); reap according to mercy and loving-kindness. Break up your uncultivated ground, for it is time to seek the Lord, to inquire for and of Him, and to require His favor, till He comes and teaches you righteousness and rains His righteous gift of salvation upon you.

HOSEA 10:12

There is never a harvest without a time of sowing (see Ecclesiastes 3:1–2). God can do anything He wants to, but He has established a life principle that works for everyone: "First you sow, and then you reap." It always happens in that order.

Those who sow trouble and mischief reap the same. Those who sow righteousness reap mercy. If God tells you to do something, and you sow obedience, and once you have passed the test, you will reap a good harvest. Remember the sequence: What you sow *today,* you will reap *tomorrow.*

Sow Generously

[Remember] this: he who sows sparingly and
grudgingly will also reap sparingly and grudgingly,
and he who sows generously [that blessings may
come to someone] will also reap generously
and with blessings.

2 CORINTHIANS 9:6

We don't sow now and reap a harvest five minutes later. We need to endure patiently in order to reap the blessing of righteousness. Ten to fifteen years may pass before a harvest comes, but God's Word is still true.

Be willing to go through the test of time in order to enjoy the harvest God promises. His Word says, "In the morning sow your seed, and in the evening withhold not your hands, for you know not which shall prosper, whether this or that, or whether both alike will be good" (Ecclesiastes 11:6). Sow good seeds generously today.

Reap the Good Life

I have told you these things, so that in Me you may have [perfect] peace and confidence. In the world you have tribulation and trials and distress and frustration; but be of good cheer [take courage; be confident, certain, undaunted]! For I have overcome the world. [I have deprived it of power to harm you and have conquered it for you.]

JOHN 16:33

God showed me that my life was in a mess because of the decisions I had made. He said, "Joyce, you have to change; start sowing good seeds, and down the road somewhere, you will reap."

If trials come against you, don't try to figure out whether you sowed some bad seeds that produced them. Trials will come, but if you will obey the Word of God long enough (not just five minutes of trial and error), sooner or later, you will come into the good life that God has prearranged for you to live.

Plant Purposefully

Do not be deceived and deluded and misled;
God will not allow Himself to be sneered at (scorned,
disdained, or mocked by mere pretensions or pro-
fessions, or by His precepts being set aside). [He
inevitably deludes himself who attempts to delude
God.] For whatever a man sows, that and that
only is what he will reap.

GALATIANS 6:7

Choose carefully what you sow through your words and actions, and plant only what you want to reap: "For he who sows to his own flesh (lower nature, sensuality) will from the flesh reap decay *and* ruin *and* destruction, but he who sows to the Spirit will from the Spirit reap eternal life" (Galatians 6:8).

Everything you do, all day long, is an opportunity to sow good seeds, or bad ones, that can drastically change things in your life. Get an early start in sowing only what you want to come back to you.

Depend on God

And I am convinced and *sure of this very thing,
that He Who began a good work in you will continue
until the day of Jesus Christ [right up to the time of
His return], developing [that good work] and perfect-
ing* and *bringing it to full completion in you.*

PHILIPPIANS 1:6

Whatever you may be struggling with today, the Holy Spirit will help you live a
self-controlled life, because the Bible says that self-
control is a fruit of the indwelling presence of the
Holy Spirit (see Galatians 5:22–23).

Allow the Holy Spirit to help you admit when
you have a problem that you need His help to overcome; then ask God for help from the Holy Spirit.

Jesus said, "Behold! I have given you authority
and power . . . and [physical and mental strength and
ability] over all the power that the enemy [possesses]"
(Luke 10:19).

God's Way Works

*Blessed (happy, fortunate, to be envied) is
everyone who fears, reveres, and worships the Lord,
who walks in His ways and lives according to
His commandments.*

PSALM 128:1

The Bible says, "Do not be deceived *and* deluded *and* misled; God will not allow Himself to be sneered at (scorned, disdained, or mocked . . . For whatever a man sows, that *and* that only is what he will reap" (Galatians 6:7). God's Word is true; He will not be mocked.

If it seems that the enemy has erected walls to keep you from your purpose, just keep doing what is right anyway. Speaking of the Lord, the psalmist says, "You have broken down all his hedges *and* his walls; You have brought his strongholds to ruin" (Psalm 89:40). God is in control; if you do right today, you will be blessed.

Keep on Keeping On

To those who by patient persistence in well-doing
[springing from piety] seek [unseen but sure]
glory and honor and [the eternal blessedness of]
immortality, He will give eternal life.

ROMANS 2:7

In Proverbs, Wisdom says: "Blessed (happy, fortunate, to be envied) is the man who listens to me, watching *daily* at my gates, waiting at the posts of my doors" (8:34). Many people seem to jump from one thing to another, when what they need is wisdom and consistency.

It is important to keep on keeping on — doing what you know is right, even if you are the only one doing it. God is on your side (see Romans 8:31), and He has already written the end of the Book. Those who obey Him will win!

Obedience Brings Success

Every Scripture is God-breathed (given by His inspiration) and profitable for instruction, for reproof and conviction of sin, for correction of error and discipline in obedience, [and] for training in righteousness (in holy living, in conformity to God's will in thought, purpose, and action).

2 TIMOTHY 3:16

The Bible says that we will reap what we sow. The dividing line between success and failure is doing what God tells us to do. We pray for fruit in our lives, but we don't always want to pray for roots.

If we want our days to go right, we need to do whatever God tells us to do. If we don't walk in obedience, then we can't complain if we wind up in a mess. If we are lonely and God tells us to invite somebody over, but we decide it is too much trouble, then we will stay lonely.

Obedience brings the fruit of the Spirit in your life. Dig deep into God's Word before you walk away from blessings today.

Jesus Is Our Standard

His intention was . . . that [we might arrive]
at really mature manhood (the completeness of
personality which is nothing less than the standard
height of Christ's own perfection), the measure of
the stature of the fullness of the Christ and the
completeness found in Him.

EPHESIANS 4:12–13

One time I was comparing myself to the way I used to be, and I thought, *I am not doing too badly.*

Then God said to me, "But Who is your standard? How are you doing compared to Me?"

I said, "Lord, I have a long way to go!"

Refuse to live beneath the standard that Jesus has set for you. Keep your eyes on Him and tell Him, "Many . . . are the wonderful works which You have done . . . no one can compare with You" (Psalm 40:5).

Receive His Grace

For we are God's [own] handiwork (His work-manship), recreated in Christ Jesus, [born anew] that we may do those good works which God predestined (planned beforehand) for us [taking paths which He prepared ahead of time], that we should walk in them [living the good life which He prearranged and made ready for us to live].

EPHESIANS 2:10

The Bible doesn't say that you have to have self-control in order to go to heaven. You are free to be out of control if you want to; it is entirely up to you. The Word does say that you have to believe that Jesus Christ is your Lord and Savior (see Romans 10:9–10).

But if you want to live the good life that God has prearranged and laid out for you before the foundation of the world, you will need to discipline yourself to do whatever His Word says to do or whatever the Holy Spirit speaks to your heart to do. God offers you the grace to live a holy life that will reap many blessings in the days to come.

Enjoy the Good Life

*You have put more joy and rejoicing in my heart
than [they know] when their wheat and new wine
have yielded abundantly. In peace I will both lie
down and sleep, for You, Lord, alone make me
dwell in safety and confident trust.*

PSALM 4:7—8

God has prearranged and made ready a good life for you, but that good life is a choice. You have to decide to follow God's leading in order to walk in it.

The Bible contains guidelines for that good life. It is not a book of laws; it is about the liberty and freedom to live the life that reaps good things. It is a book of wisdom that will lead you to peace and joy. If you do what the Word says to do, blessings will chase you and find you wherever you are (see Deuteronomy 28:1—2).

The Grace of God

*I have raised you up for this very purpose of dis-
playing My power in [dealing with] you, so that My
name may be proclaimed the whole world over.*

ROMANS 9:17

If you want victory over something, prepare yourself to work at it. But it is not a
matter of depending on yourself or winning at life
through your own determination. God gives us grace
to do good works. But grace doesn't mean that our
human flesh gets a free ride while we just lie down
and go to sleep.

You are made for good works, to be a servant of
righteousness. You are built to take responsibility,
and God will help you accomplish all He gives you
to do. He set you free from the bondage of sin so
that you can conform to His divine will in thought,
purpose, and action (see Romans 6:18). Victory is
achieved through God's grace, but you have to
choose to trust Him every step of the way.

Choose Liberty

You were washed clean (purified by a complete atonement for sin and made free from the guilt of sin), and you were consecrated (set apart, hallowed), and you were justified [pronounced righteous, by trusting] in the name of the Lord Jesus Christ and in the [Holy] Spirit of our God.

1 CORINTHIANS 6:11

As a believer, you are free to do anything you please: "All things are legitimate [permissible — and we are free to do anything we please], but not all things are helpful (expedient, profitable, and wholesome)" (1 Corinthians 10:23).

God trusts you with liberty because He has also given you a new heart full of desire to please Him. You don't have to struggle against immorality and sin when you allow Him to fill you with His Spirit each day. As a born-again, Spirit-filled believer, you have been given the liberty to lead a good life. Choose today what is wholesome, edifying, and constructive.

Accept God's Invitation

I [the Lord] will instruct you and teach you in the
way you should go; I will counsel you
with My eye upon you.

PSALM 32:8

The devil wants to keep us believers subject to legalism. If he can't condemn us for what we *do*, he will try to torment us for what we *don't do*. He wants us to feel guilty when we don't read the Word and pray, suggesting that God isn't pleased with us, or that He is even mad at us for what we *haven't done*.

God never condemns us for not being disciplined, but He lovingly invites us to spend time with Him. Heaven is available to us through simple trust in Jesus, but the good life is enjoyed when we act the way Jesus acts. We should *want to* read the Word because it holds the keys to knowing God intimately and enjoying Him fully.

Bless Yourself

I love those who love me, and those who seek me
early and diligently shall find me.

Our motives are misplaced if we think we read the Bible and pray to please God or to keep from making Him mad at us. God once told me, "You think, when you read the Bible, that you are making Me happy. I am going to be happy whether you read it or not. No, Joyce, if you read the Bible, *you're* happy. If you pray, *you're* happy. If you *give*, you *receive*."

Every single thing that God tells us to do, He tells us to do so to bless ourselves. He doesn't ask us to devote ourselves to study and prayer for Him; it is for us. The good life is our choice.

It's a Promise

Let Your mercy and *loving-kindness come*
also to me, O Lord, even Your salvation
according to Your promise.

PSALM 119:41

Some Christians want to make a law out of studying the Bible or spending a certain amount of time with God. But we should be motivated to read God's Word and spend time with Him because of our love relationship with Him, not because of a commandment to do so.

Jesus said, "If you [really] love Me, you will keep (obey) My commands" (John 14:15). What He really meant was, "If you love Me and walk in fellowship with Me, you *will* keep My commandments." If you concentrate on loving God, then keeping His commandments will become a natural part of what you do. It is a promise He makes to you.

God Does the Work

*Work out . . . your own salvation . . . [not in
your own strength] for it is God Who is all the while
effectually at work in you [energizing and creating in
you the power and desire], both to will and to work
for His good pleasure and satisfaction and delight.*

PHILIPPIANS 2:12—13

The Word of God brings liberty, not legalism; promises, not laws; and guidelines to a good life, not condemnation. Many work at following a Christian lifestyle, but they are not happy because they are focused on rules instead of on their relationship with God.

If you are trudging along, believing you *have to* give, *have to* read the Bible, *have to* pray, *have to* walk in the fruit of the Spirit, I encourage you to stop thinking you *have* to *do* anything. You will discover that God will give you the grace to *want* to do the things that lead to a victorious life in Him.

Balance Is Safety

*So everyone who hears these words of Mine
and acts upon them [obeying them] will be like
a sensible (prudent, practical, wise) man who
built his house upon the rock.*

MATTHEW 7:24

Being out of balance opens the door for the devil to rob people of the good life. The devil tempts them to live in excess and extremes. He pushes some to be workaholics and others to be lazy, whichever works to keep them unproductive. He drives some to seek wealth above God, and convinces others that poverty is godliness.

I believe that the only safe life is a balanced life. And a balanced life is obtained by keeping its priorities in line with God's truth. Build your life on solid, safe ground by praying to God and listening to His plan for you.

Live Victoriously through Moderation

Let your moderation be known unto all men.

PHILIPPIANS 4:5 KJV

God demonstrates our need for balance through the great varieties of foods He made available to us. We need some of all of it, but not all of any of it. If we overdo anything, it is just as bad as underdoing it.

Some people think, *If it is a good thing, then more of a good thing ought to be better.* But that is not necessarily true. Too much or too little can both be big problems. Balance is the key to powerful, victorious living. Ask God to show you how to stay in balance today.

Learn to Pray

Establish my steps and direct them by [means of] Your word; let not any iniquity have dominion over me. Deliver me from the oppression of man; so will I keep Your precepts [hearing, receiving, loving, and obeying them].

PSALM 119:133—134

You may pray fifteen minutes every morning, and know you are touching heaven because things happen as a result of your prayers. But if you have a friend who prays for four hours every day, you may feel that you should pray more too.

Trust God to lead you individually in how long to pray and what to pray about. Spending an extra three hours and forty-five minutes can become a work of the flesh, if you do it just to be like your friend. You can wind up miserable and unproductive if you follow what someone else is doing, instead of simply saying, "Lord, teach *me* to pray."

Show the Blessings

And the grace (unmerited favor and blessing) of our Lord [actually] flowed out superabundantly and beyond measure for me, accompanied by faith and love that are [to be realized] in Christ Jesus.

I TIMOTHY 1:14

God wants to bless you today. You may feel that you shouldn't have nice things, but let God balance your thinking when it comes to His blessings. He will help you understand what you should have and what you shouldn't have. God blesses you so that you will be a blessing to others.

When God provides for you, it offers hope to unbelievers that He is faithful to provide for those who serve Him. You are an ambassador for Christ (see 2 Corinthians 5:20); expect His provision today, and don't hide His blessings when they come.

Communicate Love

If you then, evil as you are, know how to give
good gifts [gifts that are to their advantage] to
your children, how much more will your heavenly
Father give the Holy Spirit to those who
ask and *continue to ask Him!*

LUKE 11:13

One day, my son sent me a text message on my phone while he was away on a ministry trip. It read: "Mom, I love you." That blessed me so much. Of course, the next time I went shopping, I wanted to find something for him to bless him and let him know how proud I am of him.

Send God a message today, and tell Him how much you love Him. Just like a loving parent, God enjoys meeting your needs, filling your desires, and blessing you for the love you demonstrate to Him through your obedience. He can't wait to give you what you need.

Know God's Character

*And my God will liberally supply (fill to the
full) your every need according to His
riches in glory in Christ Jesus.*

PHILIPPIANS 4:19

I believe Jesus tries to get us to sow a
good seed by making a statement that He
is first in our lives. I believe if we do that, we will receive more than we give up. I am tested in this way
all the time.

There have been many times when God has
asked me to give my last, my only, and my all. But
every time I have done so, I have ended up better off
than I was before.

Offer up your best to God today, and you will
see His character, that He is *El-Shaddai* — the God
of more than enough (see Exodus 6:3).

Imitate God's Goodness

For You make him to be blessed
and a blessing forever.

PSALM 21:6

God made a covenant with Abraham, that He would bless him, and cause him to be a blessing to others (see Genesis 12:2). You too are an heir to the true riches of God (see James 1:9). As you mature spiritually and are able to handle your inheritance, God wants you to have an abundance to bless others in His name.

Before you get involved with your daily routine today, seek God and feed your soul with His truth for your life. Experiencing God will cause you to imitate His goodness, and prosper in His abundance.

Don't Let Feelings Rule

This is my comfort and *consolation in my affliction: that Your word has revived me* and *given me life.*

God showed me that we are always going
to have feelings, and that denying the
existence of them is not godly. We do have to learn
how to manage them, so they don't manage us.

If we live by our feelings, we will be destroyed,
because our feelings aren't always in line with God's
truth. We are to walk by faith in His promises, and
not by sight or how things appear or the way we feel
(see 2 Corinthians 5:7). Ask God to keep your feelings balanced with the truth of His Word today.

Temptation Isn't Sin

In the day when I called, You answered me; and
You strengthened me with strength (might and inflex-
ibility to temptation) in my inner self.

PSALM 138:3

Temptation to do wrong can make you feel horrible. You may think, *I shouldn't be going through this; I shouldn't be having a problem with this.* But God taught me that temptation isn't sin; we sin when we give in to temptation.

The Bible says temptation will come. It doesn't say, "Woe unto him to whom it comes," it says, "Woe unto him by whose hand it comes" (see Matthew 17:7). Jesus told us to pray that we would not give in to the temptation when we are tempted (see Luke 22:40).

Psalm 105:4 is a great way to start your day right. It says, "Seek, inquire of *and* for the Lord, *and* crave Him and His strength (His might and inflexibility to temptation); seek *and* require His face *and* His presence [continually] evermore."

Forgiveness Wins

For if you forgive people their trespasses [their reckless and willful sins, leaving them, letting them go, and giving up resentment], your heavenly Father will also forgive you.

MATTHEW 6:14

Unforgiveness will ruin your day. If someone hurts you, pray quickly, "God, I forgive them in Jesus' name." If your emotions feel strained when you see that person, stand firm in your decision to forgive them.

Pray for them, asking God to show you how to bless them. Do whatever God leads you to do for them, and let God's love work through you to heal the rift between you. If you do your part, God will bring your feelings in line with your decision, and you will enjoy your day and your life.

Be Truthful

*Do not say, I will repay evil; wait [expectantly]
for the Lord, and He will rescue you.*

PROVERBS 20:22

God doesn't mind if you tell Him how you honestly feel. Actually, telling God how you feel will give you relief. If you repress your feelings and pretend you aren't angry or hurting, and try to be superspiritual, you will miss the healing that God can give to you.

Be truthful with God. Don't carry a grudge all day. Get in touch with what is going on inside of you and talk to God about it. Truth is the only thing that will set you free to enjoy the rest of your day (see John 8:32).

Get Over It

Open rebuke is better than love that is hidden.

PROVERBS 27:5

Hiding your true feelings, like resentment or unforgiveness, keeps you in bondage to them. It is impossible to get your day started right if you keep waking up with pain from yesterday's wounds. If you carry around this kind of "emotional baggage," it will poison your day.

Sometimes you have to confront things to make them better. But use wisdom. While it is good to talk about things, don't dump all your thoughts and emotions on every person who comes along today.

Talk to God about your situation before you meet anyone. He may lead you to speak with someone you trust. But if He doesn't, learn to trust it completely to Him, and let it go.

Minister to Your Emotions

Keep and *protect me, O God, for in You
I have found refuge,* and *in You do I put
my trust* and *hide myself.*

PSALM 16:1

God gave us feelings, and it is all right to minister to your emotions or to the emotions of other people. Do something kind for yourself to keep your emotions healthy; just don't be ruled by them.

Treat yourself to a hot bath or a walk in the fresh air. Do what you need to do to get emotional release. If yesterday wore you out, get refreshed spiritually and emotionally before starting a new day. Find some time alone with God, listen to teaching or music tapes, and refill your heart with an awareness of God's presence.

Find Balance

*Since all this is true, we ought to pay much
closer attention than ever to the truths
that we have heard, lest in any way we drift past
[them] and slip away.*

HEBREWS 2:1

When Satan finds people out of balance, he has an inroad to destroy their lives. There are people who get out of balance in everything: from not sleeping, to sleeping too much; from not cleaning their house, to trying to keep it so clean that nobody can move in it.

Find balance; balance keeps your day going right. Satan doesn't much care if you don't do enough of something, or if you do too much of it, as long as you don't stay balanced. Take time to examine yourself prayerfully, and ask God to show you how to remain balanced.

Appreciate Your Calling

*So we, numerous as we are, are one body in Christ
(the Messiah) and individually we are parts one of
another [mutually dependent on one another].*

ROMANS 12:5

Learn to appreciate the call of God on
your life. He has a different call for everybody. None of us are called to do *all* the work that
needs to be done, but we can each enjoy the assignments we are given. We can also enjoy the work
God does through others.

Today holds an opportunity to mature in the
knowledge of God and to enjoy whatever God has
called you to do. Your part is needed. Ask God early
in the day to show you where to use your gifts to
help others.

Speak Positively

Behold, You desire truth in the inner being; make me therefore to know wisdom in my inmost heart.

PSALM 51:6

Focus on speaking words in faith today; keep your confession truthful but positive. Don't deny the existence of your circumstances, but confess what God's Word has to say about your situation.

For example, if you are sneezing, coughing, and finding it difficult to breathe, it isn't truthful to say you aren't sick. But you can learn to present a negative situation in a positive way. You can say, "I believe God's healing power is working in me, and that I am getting better all the time."

Avoid Extremes

Apply your mind to instruction and correction and your ears to words of knowledge.

PROVERBS 23:12

When I first became a Christian, I heard a message about keeping my mouth shut, so I made a decision that the next day I wouldn't open my mouth to say anything. I was determined not to get myself in any trouble with my words.

The next morning I did not say a word for several hours. Then somebody asked me, "What is your problem?" That made me mad all over again. Eventually I learned that extremes never make our days go right. Reading God's Word helps us find balance to face everything that comes our way. The Word says we are to be *well-balanced* because the devil seeks someone to devour (see 1 Peter 5:8).

Unseen Promises Exist

*And whatever you ask for in prayer, having faith
and [really] believing, you will receive.*

MATTHEW 21:22

Before the fulfillment of God's promise to multiply Abram, He changed his name from Abram ("high exalted father") to Abraham, ("father of a multitude") (see Genesis 17:1–6). God spoke the promise long before it was visible to anyone.

Anything that is in the Word of God is a promise that be can rightfully and legally spoken forth even before it visibly exists. Reach into the spiritual realm, that you cannot see, and pull the promises of God out of there, with the words of your mouth, and prophesy them into existence. Read God's Word and speak as the Holy Spirit leads you to do so today.

God's Word Changes Things

*Yet we have the same spirit of faith as he had who
wrote, I have believed, and therefore have I spoken.
We too believe, and therefore we speak.*

2 CORINTHIANS 4:13

God created with words everything that
we see. God *said,* "Let there be light," and
there was light. Hebrews 11:3 says that everything
that is visible was made from the invisible. God has
blessings stored up for you in the spiritual realm that
you may not be experiencing, but they do exist.

Speak positive words today, and call those things
that are not (that are invisible) into your life (see
Romans 4:17). If you face a problem today, say, "My
problem is temporary. God's Word says that I am an
overcomer because of Christ's love for me. Even
though I don't see the answers now, God will provide for all of my needs."

Esteem Others

*Let each one of us make it a practice to please
(make happy) his neighbor for his good and for his
true welfare, to edify him [to strengthen him and
build him up spiritually].*

ROMANS 15:2

There are people who make "ministries" out of criticizing everybody else. But most people who judge others who are actually doing something are the ones who are doing nothing themselves. They put down other people to try to lift up themselves.

The Word of God calls us to build up others, esteeming them more highly than ourselves (see Philippians 2:3). Avoid people who constantly criticize others so their negative comments will not rob you of godly enthusiasm. God can use you today to help strengthen someone's faith. Ask Him to make you aware of these opportunities today.

Love Truth

Instead, speaking the truth in love, we will in
all things grow up into him who is
the Head, that is, Christ.

EPHESIANS 4:15 NIV

If you want to become fully mature in the Lord, you must learn to love truth. Otherwise, you will always leave open a door of deception for the enemy to take what is meant to be yours.

Some people have a difficult time facing truth and reality. They prefer to live in a make-believe world, pretending that certain things aren't happening. But we cannot deny the existence of problems or act as if they are not real.

The devil is real, life is real, people are real, pain is real, and poverty is real. The good news is that no matter how real our pain may be, or how big our problems may seem, we can overcome all of them with the Word of God.

Enjoy Your Whole Day

I will praise You, O Lord, with my whole heart;
I will show forth (recount and tell aloud) all Your
marvelous works and wonderful deeds!

PSALM 9:1

Some Christians feel guilty when they are doing something that isn't "spiritual." Somehow or another, they feel the need to hurry through the grocery store, dash through the house cleaning, and rush through all the daily aspects of life that seem irrelevant to their faith. They want to get back to doing something "spiritual" so God will be pleased with them again.

God did not intend for you to *hate* the secular side of life. You can enjoy *holiness* and time with God even when you are doing daily chores, running errands, or taking the children somewhere they need to go. Don't begrudge the routine things of life; see every activity as an opportunity to serve God with your whole heart.

Encourage, Don't Criticize

*Therefore encourage (admonish, exhort) one an-
other and edify (strengthen and build up) one another.*

1 THESSALONIANS 5:11

We can improve our relationships with others by leaps and bounds if we become encouragers instead of critics. It is the greater person who does the right thing; Christ's righteousness dwells in you to help you do what is right. You are great in God's eyes when you choose to do right and bless others.

No matter how rough your day is today, speak words that uplift and encourage those around you. Encourage others if you notice them doing a good job — not just those who work with you, but people wherever you go, such as store clerks, auto mechanics, and waiters. Say something like, "I appreciate the extra effort you are making to do your job well." You can change your life and someone else's by choosing to speak positive words.

Keep Balanced

For we who have believed (adhered to and trusted in and relied on God) do enter that rest.

HEBREWS 4:3

It is easy to get overcommitted, burned out, bummed out, worn out, and stressed out if you are trying to keep up with too many commitments. It is out of balance to try to do everything. If you are happy doing what you do, keep doing it. But if it wears you out and robs you of peace, don't do it. What sense does it make to commit to something, and then murmur and complain about it while you are doing it?

Being overcommitted will frustrate you. Anxiety is usually a sign that God never told you to do what you are doing in the first place. To avoid frustration in your life, keep in balance.

Talk to God Anywhere

Do you not know that your body is the temple (the very sanctuary) of the Holy Spirit Who lives within you, Whom you have received [as a Gift] from God?

1 CORINTHIANS 6:19

The angel of the Lord said to Moses, "Take the shoes off your feet, for the ground on which you stand is holy ground" (see Exodus 3:5). The ground was holy because the Holy One was there. Now through faith in Jesus, you are the temple of the Holy Ghost. Everywhere you go becomes a holy place because the Holy One dwells in you.

God is not in a building, where you can only visit Him on Sunday morning. He is with you everywhere you go. You can talk to Him while you vacuum, or while you change the oil in your car. When you let God become involved in every aspect of your life, every day becomes exciting.

Pray All Day

Let my prayer be set forth as incense before You,
the lifting up of my hands as the evening sacrifice.

PSALM 141:2

God wants to be the center of your life: the center of your conversation, the center of your entertainment, and the center of your relationships. Prayer keeps Him in the center of all you do.

Years ago I could have told you that I prayed an hour every day. But now, I couldn't even determine how long I pray, because I just pray every time I see or feel a need. I pray while driving. I pray while working, and while relaxing. Sometimes I just stop what I am doing and praise God, and that is prayer too. I cast my cares on Him and say, "Lord, I am not going to worry about anything today; I am giving it to You."

Prayer should be like breathing, natural to do anywhere you are.

Loving Actions Speak Clearly

[Living as becomes you] with complete lowliness of mind (humility) and meekness (unselfishness, gentleness, mildness), with patience, bearing with one another and making allowances because you love one another

EPHESIANS 4:2

It is good for the unsaved members of your family to see you studying the Bible, going to church, and bearing the fruit of the Spirit. But your family may be more receptive to the gospel if you minister to their needs. Ministering to them may require giving up a prayer meeting to do things with them, such as going fishing or shopping with your spouse, helping your son work on his car, or taking your daughter out for lunch.

The Bible says that the natural man does not understand the spiritual man (see 1 Corinthians 2:14). So spiritual talk doesn't always make sense to unsaved people, but loving actions speak clearly to them. Walk in love's anointing today: be kind, joyful, peaceful, and stable. Let God love others through you.

Be Wise to the Enemy

Be well balanced . . . for that enemy of yours, the devil, roams around like a lion roaring . . . seeking someone to seize upon and devour.

1 PETER 5:8

Satan cannot devour just anybody he pleases. He has to find someone who gives him an opening to do so. One of the ways we give him an opening to destroy us is through imbalance in our lives. A good example would be, if we eat improperly and in an unbalanced manner over a long period of time, we may open the door for the enemy to bring sickness or disease into our life.

Many times when people are recovering from illness, they follow a strict diet that brings balance back into their eating habits. Find balance in all you do, and keep the enemy away from your door.

Internal Blessings Show Externally

Therefore if any person is [ingrafted] in Christ
(the Messiah) he is a new creation (a new creature
altogether); the old [previous moral and spiritual
condition] has passed away. Behold, the
fresh and new has come!

2 CORINTHIANS 5:17

When God baptized me in the Holy Ghost, I felt like He had filled me with liquid love. He did something on the inside of me, and it showed on the outside of me. Internal changes last, and keep showing up in everything we do.

That is why you can't really be a closet Christian. If you are saved, it will show to others. If you say you are saved, but nothing has changed in your life, something is wrong. When Jesus comes to live in you, He will get involved with how you live and how you look at life to make you more like Him. Welcome any changes He needs to make in you today.

Talk about God — Not the Devil

Leave no [such] room or foothold for the devil [give no opportunity to him].

EPHESIANS 4:27

God once said to me, "Quit talking so much about the devil, what he is saying and what he is doing. *I am* saying something! Talk about what I am saying. *I am* doing something! Talk about what *I am* doing."

Then one day God spoke a *life-changing* word to me, saying, "Why don't you study the Word, and see how Jesus waged spiritual warfare?"

I found that Jesus didn't talk or preach much about the devil and what he was saying or doing. He simply dealt with the devil by casting him out of people's lives. He told him to shut up. He quoted the Word to him (see Luke 4:1–13). Resist the devil today and tell someone about the good things God is doing for you.

Hold on to Your Peace

In His [Christ's] days shall the [uncompromis-
ingly] righteous flourish and peace abound till
there is a moon no longer.

PSALM 72:7

In the Bible, people are told to hold their peace, because peace is a place of power. God tells us not to be moved when our opponents and adversaries come against us. We are to remain constant, fearless, and at peace. His Word says, "The Lord will fight for you, and you shall hold your peace *and* remain at rest" (Exodus 14:14).

No matter what is happening, remain consistent; continue treating people well, continue walking in the fruit of the Spirit. You don't know what kind of fruit you have until somebody comes along and squeezes it. You don't know how much fruit you have until somebody is picking it all day.

Do What Is Right

*Trust (lean on, rely on, and be confident) in the
Lord and do good; so shall you dwell in the land
and feed surely on His faithfulness, and
truly you shall be fed.*

PSALM 37:3

Powerful results happen when you do
what is right. Doing what is right is high-
tech spiritual warfare! It puts you in a position where
the devil can't affect you, because you have decided
to stand and not be moved.

Remain in faith and trust God. The Bible says in
Psalm 37:1 that evildoers, "those who work unrighteousness (that which is not upright or in right
standing with God)," will be cut down like the grass.
When problems arise against you, when your enemies attack you, or when evil makes an all-out as-
sault upon you, trust in the Lord, and do good.

Don't Lose Focus

For the weapons of our warfare are not physical
[weapons of flesh and blood], but they are mighty
before God for the overthrow and
destruction of strongholds.

2 CORINTHIANS 10:4

Sometimes we lose our focus. We can be walking in love all day, going along fine, until someone comes along and offends us. As soon as we forget our focus of love, we stop making progress and come to a standstill — aggravated, upset, and offended.

Understand that the mind is a battlefield. If you don't stop Satan when he gets into your thoughts, you are not going to stop him from getting into your life. Stay focused. Ask God to help you remain full of love, no matter what comes your way today.

Build on Solid Foundations

For no other foundation can anyone lay than that which is [already] laid, which is Jesus Christ (the Messiah, the Anointed One).

1 CORINTHIANS 3:11

We can know a lot of spiritual methods (or formulas) for getting things, but many such methods simply have no power flowing through them. Powerless methods are like empty containers — useless.

I had learned many spiritual methods, and I was busy trying them, until I realized that methods don't work. It was like building on a cracked foundation; nothing stood the test of time. If our foundations leak, we get into trouble every time it storms.

Build your life on who you are in Christ. Take time to meditate on the foundational things about being a Christian. Build your life on the solid foundation that you are an heir of God's grace and His unmerited favor.

Be Confident in God

For the Lord shall be your confidence, firm and
strong, and shall keep your foot from being caught
[in a trap or some hidden danger].

PROVERBS 3:26

Jesus knew where He came from, He knew what He was sent to do, and He knew where He was going. When you get that confidence of knowing God and His purpose for your life, you will not be affected by the judgments or criticisms of other people.

You know you belong to God. You know His hand is on you. You know His anointing is on you. You know what you are called to do. You know that with every breath you take, you are trying to follow Him, and you know where you are going when you are all finished. Say, "Nothing that happens today can separate me from God's love and His purpose for my life."

God's Promises
Will Be Fulfilled

*Little children, you are of God [you belong
to Him] and have [already] defeated and overcome
them [the agents of the antichrist], because He Who
lives in you is greater (mightier) than he
who is in the world.*

1 JOHN 4:4

Know who you are in Christ and understand that through salvation, you are seen
in the spiritual world as wearing a garment of salvation and covered with a robe of righteousness (see
Isaiah 61:10). God is on your side, and He is under
you, over you, around you, with you, for you, and
in you.

The devil *knows* you belong to Christ because
God "[has also appropriated and acknowledged us as
His by] putting His seal upon us and giving us His
[Holy] Spirit in our hearts as the security deposit
and guarantee [of the fulfillment of His promise]"
(2 Corinthians 1:22).

Powerful Christianity

But you will receive power when the Holy Spirit
comes on you; and you will be my witnesses in
Jerusalem, and in all Judea and Samaria, and
to the ends of the earth.

ACTS 1:8 NIV

Being *Spirit-filled* is not limited to one particular brand of Christianity. Spirit-filled people are found in every church and denomination. They are people who understand the need for the power of the Holy Ghost within them so they won't live a weak, defeated life.

The Word says to "ever be filled *and* stimulated with the [Holy] Spirit" (Ephesians 5:18), indicating that being Spirit-filled is something to which we submit ourselves. Ask God to fill you to overflowing with His Spirit so that everything you do today will be done through His power.

Stay in God's Presence

*And now shall my head be lifted up above my
enemies round about me; in His tent I will offer
sacrifices* and *shouting of joy; I will sing, yes,
I will sing praises to the Lord.*

PSALM 27:6

The psalmist David said that the thing he
wanted most was to be with God and to
dwell in His presence all the days of his life (see
Psalm 27:4). David loved God for who He is, not
just for what He did for him.

The Word says that if we abide in the presence
of God, He will defeat our enemies, and hide us in
the day of trouble (see v. 5). God's attention is on us,
but we must keep our attention on Him to enjoy the
fullness of His presence in our lives. We must invite
God to be involved in everything we do, and then
remember to praise Him for His goodness.

Seek God First

[After all] the kingdom of God is not a matter of
[getting the] food and drink [one likes], but instead
it is righteousness (that state which makes a person
acceptable to God) and [heart] peace and joy in
the Holy Spirit. He who serves Christ in this way
is acceptable and *pleasing to God and is*
approved by men.

ROMANS 14:17—18

Forget all the *things* you think you need, and just admit to God that you need *Him*. Seek first the kingdom of God and His righteousness, and all that you need will be added to your life (see Matthew 6:33).

God knows your needs even before you ask. Don't become a seeker of promotion or position. Don't spend your life seeking prosperity. Seek the One who prospers. Seek the One who heals. Seek the One who is the giver of every good and perfect gift.

Remain Steadfast

And he [Abram] believed in (trusted in, relied on,
remained steadfast to) the Lord, and He counted it to
him as righteousness (right standing with God).

GENESIS 15:6

Spending time with God keeps you stable, steadfast, and calm. God says He "will strengthen and harden you to difficulties" (Isaiah 41:10). When your faith is fed daily by God's presence, the devil can't control you, because you don't get easily upset.

Being filled with God's truth makes it easier to live the life God has for you. Let God be your anchor in the midst of the raging waves of circumstances. Remain steadfast in God.

Don't Be Entangled

Put on God's whole armor [the armor of a heavy-armed soldier which God supplies], that you may be able successfully to stand up against [all] the strategies and the deceits of the devil.

EPHESIANS 6:11

We are called to be soldiers in the army of God. Paul told Timothy that no soldier gets entangled with civilian affairs, but "his aim is to satisfy *and* please the one who enlisted him" (2 Timothy 2:4). Likewise, as we serve the Lord, we should focus on His work, not our own concerns.

If we want to be a witness of God's power, we must first do what He says to do, and show others the fruit that comes from serving Him (see vv. 6–7). We do this by keeping our minds constantly on Jesus Christ. We must still handle the business of everyday life, but we are not to let the affairs of the world pull us down.

It's the Lord's Battle

*The Angel of the Lord encamps around those
who fear Him [who revere and worship Him
with awe] and each of them He delivers.*

PSALM 34:7

In the Old Testament, people carried banners when they went to war, sending the singers and praisers into the battle first. When the tribe of Judah sang, "Oh, give thanks to the Lord, for He is good, for His mercy endures forever" (see 2 Chronicles 20:21), the enemy was so confused they were self-slaughtered and self-defeated (see v. 22).

When King Jehoshaphat prepared for battle, he took the position of getting on his face to worship God (see v. 18). If you have battles to face, get in the position of warfare, and just worship the Lord. God's response to our worship is, "Be not afraid or dismayed at this great multitude; for the battle is not yours, but God's" (v. 15).

Spiritual Warfare

And let the peace (soul harmony which comes)
from Christ rule (act as umpire continually) in your
hearts [deciding and settling with finality all ques-
tions that arise in your minds, in that peaceful
state] . . . And be thankful (appreciative),
[giving praise to God always].

COLOSSIANS 3:15

You are waging spiritual warfare when you give radical praise to God in the midst of your need and lack. When you are thankful to God for all He has done and is doing, you are defeating the enemy. When you hold your peace in the midst of the storm, you are warring with spiritual weapons (see 2 Corinthians 10:4–5).

Jesus said, "Peace I leave with you; My [own] peace I now give *and* bequeath to you . . . [Stop allowing yourselves to be agitated and disturbed; and do not permit yourselves to be fearful and intimidated and cowardly and unsettled]" (John 14:27). Jesus has given you peace! Put it on, and wear it everywhere you go.

Stand!

*[Earnestly] remember the former things, [which I
did] of old; for I am God, and there is no one else;
I am God, and there is none like Me, declaring the
end* and *the result from the beginning, and from
ancient times the things that are not yet done,
saying, My counsel shall stand, and I will
do all My pleasure* and *purpose.*

ISAIAH 46:9–10

There may be times when it seems that
you cannot go forward, but at least you
do not have to go backward. You may not know how
to forge ahead, but you can stand firmly on what you
know of God.

Instead of passively yielding to the enemy, you
can say, "This is the ground I have gained, and I am
not giving it up, devil. You are not driving me back
into the hole that God pulled me out of. I am going
to stand strong in the power of God until He delivers me."

Submit Yourself to God

My soul, wait only upon God and *silently submit
to Him; for my hope* and *expectation are from Him.*

PSALM 62:5

James 4:7–8 gives the best advice on how to wage spiritual warfare: "Be subject to God. Resist the devil [stand firm against him], and he will flee from you. Come close to God and He will come close to you."

When you humble yourself in the presence of the Lord, He will exalt you and lift you and make your life significant (see vv. 9–10). God will show you how to resist the devil. Spend time in God's presence, and do whatever He tells you to do!

Don't Stay Angry

Cease from anger and forsake wrath; fret not yourself — it tends only to evildoing.

PSALM 37:8

The Word tells us another way to resist temptation: "When angry, do not sin; do not ever let your wrath (your exasperation, your fury or indignation) last until the sun goes down. Leave no [such] room or foothold for the devil [give no opportunity to him]" (Ephesians 4:26–27).

Paul said that we should forgive people to keep Satan from gaining an advantage over us (see 2 Corinthians 2:10–11). If someone offends you, get over it quickly so you won't leave open a door for the devil. It is a sin to hold anger and bitterness, so never go to sleep mad. If you forgive everyone before you fall asleep, freedom from wrong attitudes in your heart will help you start your day right the next morning.

Go on Through

Yes, though I walk through the [deep, sunless]
valley of the shadow of death, I will fear or dread no
evil, for You are with me; Your rod [to protect] and
Your staff [to guide], they comfort me.

PSALM 23:4

Knowing God personally requires trusting Him through the hard times in life and not running away from trials. It requires being faithful to do whatever He says to do, being steadfast while waiting for Him to work out your problems.

You understand how faithful and how good God is when you see His deliverance in your life. You can't get that certainty by reading a book about Him. Your faith increases by *going through* tough times and seeing His presence make a difference in your life. Don't run away from God during tests and trials; draw near to Him, and listen for His voice of assurance.

Be Determined

Even when we were dead (slain) by [our own]
shortcomings and trespasses, He made us alive
together in fellowship and in union with Christ;
[He gave us the very life of Christ Himself, the same
new life with which He quickened Him, for] it is
by grace (His favor and mercy which you did not
deserve) that you are saved (delivered from judgment
and made partakers of Christ's salvation).

EPHESIANS 2:5

Paul said, "My determined purpose is,
that I may know Christ, and the power of
His resurrection, the power that lifts me out from
among the dead, even while I am in the body" (see
Philippians 3:10–11).

You can use every day to get to know God in a
deeper way. Read the Bible for understanding of what
He wants to reveal to you, and receive His grace to
be lifted out of every past fault. Let His power lift
you into life His way.

Don't Get Rattled

Just think of Him Who endured from sinners such grievous opposition and bitter hostility against Himself [reckon up and consider it all in comparison with your trials], so that you may not grow weary or exhausted, losing heart and relaxing and fainting in your minds.

HEBREWS 12:3

We have authority over the devil, but that doesn't mean he will never come against us. Resisting the devil doesn't rid us of the problem. But standing in the faith of God's promises while we are waiting for God to do something keeps us from *acting like* the devil ourselves.

Don't get rattled about the devil. If he causes problems for you today, just say, "Forget it, devil! I am not staying hurt, bitter, wounded, or angry. My trust is in God. I am a Christian — watch me be happy."

Let Christ Live Through You

*The life I now live in the body I live by faith
in (by adherence to and reliance on and complete
trust in) the Son of God, Who loved me and gave
Himself up for me.*

GALATIANS 2:20

Some people need to unlearn some things before they can start learning what God wants for them. For example, some people try to manipulate others with their self-pity or anger. They believe these emotional tools will get what they want from others. Some people who have been hurt or abused feel that they have to take care of themselves because nobody else will.

Both attitudes display the common fear, "What about me? What about me?" But Paul offers us a life-changing principle to follow: "I have been crucified with Christ and I no longer live, but Christ lives in me" (Galatians 2:20 NIV). When Christ lives through you, you will enjoy every day of your life.

Trust God

But let all those who take refuge and *put their trust in You rejoice; let them ever sing* and *shout for joy, because You make a covering over them* and *defend them; let those also who love Your name be joyful in You* and *be in high spirits.*

PSALM 5:11

Many wounded people don't know how to get what they really need, so they wallow in self-pity. God once told me, "Joyce, you can be pitiful or powerful, but you can't be both."

Taking our eyes off of ourselves enables us to look to God. This positions us to trust Him to meet every need in our lives. God knows exactly what we need, and He promises to provide it through His abundant grace and mercy.

Ask Him to fill you with His power today, and trust Him as *Jehovah-Jireh,* the Lord our Provider (see Genesis 22:14 KJV).

Wait for God's Justice

*Knowing [with all certainty] that it is from the
Lord [and not from men] that you will receive the
inheritance which is your [real] reward. [The One
Whom] you are actually serving [is] the Lord
Christ (the Messiah).*

COLOSSIANS 3:24

God has brought a great reward in my life
in recompense for the abuse that I suffered in my earlier days. Now I have a wonderful
life. God blesses me. He does things for me. He opens
doors of opportunity for me. He makes me happy.
He gives me joy.

When you really trust God, He will bring justice
into your life. In Isaiah 61:7 the Lord says, "For your
former shame I will give you a double reward" (paraphrased). If someone has mistreated you, rejected
you, abused you, or abandoned you, hold on to that
promise. You have many blessings ahead of you.
Trust God with your future, and enjoy your day as
you wait for God's justice.

Choose to Be Changed

*But we have the mind of Christ (the Messiah) and
do hold the thoughts (feelings and
purposes) of His heart.*

1 CORINTHIANS 2:16

Do you get mad every time somebody
tries to correct you, or tell you what to
do, because you always have to be right? If you answered yes, I am sure that you are not a happy person. You cannot change others, but you can allow God to change you so that things don't bother you anymore.

With Jesus Christ as your Savior, you can learn how to live a different way. You can have peace. You can sleep well at night. You can like yourself. You can restore relationships that have been ruined. Your mind can be renewed to be like Jesus', if you read His Word and ask Him to help you live the abundant life He came to give you (see John 10:10).

Use Your Authority Well

*Whoever wishes to be great among you must be
your servant, and whoever desires to be first among
you must be your slave — just as the Son of Man
came not to be waited on but to serve, and to
give His life as a ransom for many [the
price paid to set them free].*

MATTHEW 20:26–28

God desires to restore us to our rightful position of authority in Christ. But first, we must learn to respect authority before we are fit to be in authority.

We all have authorities to whom God expects us to submit. Our government, our law officers, and even our merchants have the right to set rules for us to follow. If we are not submitting to God's appointed authority, it will soon be revealed.

Keep a submissive attitude in your heart, and enjoy the authority you have been given to spend time in God's presence today.

Change Things with Knowledge

Commit your way to the Lord [roll and repose each care of your load on Him]; trust (lean on, rely on, and be confident) also in Him and He will bring it to pass.

PSALM 37:5

We are all eager for our situations and relationships to change, but nothing will change in our lives without knowledge of God's Word. In Hosea 4:6 God says, "My people are destroyed for lack of knowledge."

Change comes through prayer, and then through waiting patiently on God. While we are waiting for God to solve our problems, we are not to complain to everybody else about our situation.

God tells us to trust Him. He is not asking us to trust the people involved in our problems; He is asking us to trust Him. There is a difference. He is faithful to rescue us from all our troubles.

Lend a Helping Hand

He who is greatest among you
shall be your servant.

MATTHEW 23:11

If we help someone become what God wants them to be, God will send someone along to help us be everything God wants us to be.

One day I asked one of our musicians if he would like to do something that needed to be done. He said, "I will do whatever you tell me to do; I am here to serve you."

I said, "But do you *want* to do this? You don't have to do it; we can find someone else."

He said, "It doesn't matter if I want to or not. Tell me what you want me to do, and I will do it." He was anointed to help others and enjoyed doing whatever needed to be done.

To enjoy your day, be ready to help people with whatever God has called them to do.

Opportunity Brings Opposition

But he who looks carefully into the faultless law, the [law] of liberty, and is faithful to it and perseveres in looking into it, being not a heedless listener who forgets but an active doer [who obeys], he shall be blessed in his doing (his life of obedience).

JAMES 1:25

Many people agree with a sermon or a Scripture, but they don't apply it in their everyday life, so nothing changes. They think that just because they agree with the Word, it should bring change into their life.

But change doesn't happen automatically; a person has to be a *doer* of the Word, not a hearer only. Jesus said, "Keep awake (give strict attention, be cautious and active) *and* watch and pray, that you may not come into temptation. The spirit indeed is willing, but the flesh is weak" (Matthew 26:41).

Every time you have an opportunity to believe God for something, you will have a temptation to give up on it. Pray that you will overcome temptation when it comes.

Enjoy Liberty

Blessed (happy, to be envied) is the man who is
patient under trial and stands up under temptation,
for when he has stood the test and been approved,
he will receive [the victor's] crown of life which
God has promised to those who love Him.

JAMES 1:12

Life is miserable when we won't listen to anybody else, or when we get mad every time somebody doesn't agree with us. To be so emotionally ruled and controlled that we are stressed every time something doesn't go our way is bondage. When Jesus sets us free, it means that we are free *not* to get upset just because we don't get everything we want.

It is wonderful to be free. We can give thanks for the liberty to receive God's help and walk in patience despite our circumstances. Our lives can be happy, blessed, and peaceful. We can experience joy no matter what the situation may be.

Enjoy a New Beginning

But there is forgiveness with You
[just what man needs], that You may be
reverently feared and worshiped.

PSALM 130:4

People sometimes tell me, "I did something wrong, and I just don't know if God can ever forgive me of it." Even when we have made serious mistakes, there is always a place of forgiveness and a new beginning in Christ. When we have a new beginning with Christ, we don't have to mourn over the past. We just have to repent and go on. We don't need to repent again and again.

If you know the character of God, you know He will forgive any sin, no matter how terrible, because to Him sin is sin. Remember, God can make miracles out of mistakes. If you need forgiveness today, simply confess to the Lord what you have done, and enjoy your new beginning (see 1 John 1:9). It begins at the moment of forgiveness.

Accept Responsibility

Finally, brethren, farewell (rejoice)! Be strengthened (perfected, completed, made what you ought to be); be encouraged and consoled and comforted; be of the same [agreeable] mind one with another; live in peace, and [then] the God of love [Who is the Source of affection, goodwill, love, and benevolence toward men] and the Author and Promoter of peace will be with you.

2 CORINTHIANS 13:11

Each one of us needs to accept our responsibility to do what is right in God's eyes, whether others do the right thing or not. Otherwise we will have a standoff:

"Well, if you won't say you're sorry, then I won't say I'm sorry."

"You're not nice, so I'm not going to be nice."

"You haven't given me a compliment in a year, so I'm not giving you one either."

That attitude gets relationships in trouble. God wants us to live above the pettiness of selfish arguments by loving one another.

Start Something

*[Let your] love be sincere (a real thing); hate
what is evil [loathe all ungodliness, turn in horror
from wickedness], but hold fast to that which is
good. Love one another with brotherly affection
[as members of one family], giving precedence and
showing honor to one another. Never lag in zeal
and in earnest endeavor; be aglow and burning
with the Spirit, serving the Lord.*

ROMANS 12:9—11

If all of us started having a godly attitude,
it would catch hold and spread like a virus. Wouldn't it be great if we could spread a good
virus?

Imagine the whispers: "Have you heard? There's
something wonderful going around. Have you caught
it? It is running rampant all over the place. Everywhere you look, people have a *new attitude!*"

Let's start something today! Let's decide to think
like Christ. Let's decide to love everyone we meet
today, and pass the word so that everybody catches
on to it.

Start Something Good

*For there shall the seed produce peace and
prosperity; the vine shall yield her fruit and the
ground shall give its increase and the heavens
shall give their dew; and I will cause the remnant of
this people to inherit and possess all these things.*

ZECHARIAH 8:12

Start something good in someone's life
today. Sow faith for a healing. Sow hope
for a restoration. A sincere compliment can sow
confidence in someone who is starving for encouragement. Your forgiveness of an ongoing offense can
sow a seed for a miracle breakthrough in that situation.

Pray for someone else's need, or make a special
offering to start something positive in the name of
the Lord. Remember, God won't ask you to sow
anything that He doesn't give you the grace to give.
Enjoy the abundant harvest that is returned to your
own life when you sow into someone else's life.

Be Christ's Bond Servant

Now the Lord is the Spirit, and where the Spirit of
the Lord is, there is liberty (emancipation
from bondage, freedom).

2 CORINTHIANS 3:17

Paul said that he would not become the slave of anything or anyone but Jesus Christ: "Everything is lawful for me, but I will not become the slave of anything *or* be brought under its power" (1 Corinthians 6:12)." He also said, "If I had been trying to be popular with people, I would not now be a bond servant of the Lord Jesus Christ" (see Galatians 1:10).

If you let other people control you, you will not fulfill the call of God on your life. If you let their rejection frighten you and change your focus, you won't do what God wants you to do. Be a slave only to God, and a servant to people on His behalf.

Follow Jesus

All who keep His commandments [who obey His orders and follow His plan, live and continue to live, to stay and] abide in Him, and He in them. [They let Christ be a home to them and they are the home of Christ.]

1 JOHN 3:24

Some people wanted to follow Jesus, but they were afraid they would be put out of the synagogue (see John 12:42). Some people are still afraid to follow the Lord because they might be put out of their family, their group, or even their church.

Eventually, there will only be one Person to face — God. You won't want Him to say, "I had so much for you, but you didn't receive it because you were too concerned about what people thought; you were a people-pleaser." Jesus wasn't swayed by men's opinions, threats, judgments, or criticisms. Follow Jesus, and enjoy life.

Listen to God

Hear counsel, receive instruction, and *accept correction, that you may be wise in the time to come.*

PROVERBS 19:20

You may wonder, "How do I know when to confront someone about an issue, and when to let it go?" If you are too eager to set someone straight, it may not be God motivating you. Correction must be done in love to build up the person and not tear them down. Always pray and wait until you know what God wants you to do.

You must be led of the Spirit. If after prayer you still feel that you are to talk to someone about their behavior, be absolutely sure that you are doing it for their good and not yours. If it is what God has told you to do, you may not even want to do it, but it will be done as an act of obedience to Him. Whatever you do, do it in love.

Don't Get Burned Out

*And be constantly renewed in the spirit of your
mind [having a fresh mental and spiritual attitude].*

EPHESIANS 4:23

Expect God to show you something new
today. Some people resist change, but
God created us to need variety in our life. If we do
the same thing over and over, we get burned out on
it. God will keep our lives exciting if we seek Him
every day.

Look for new ways of doing things. If you have
been working on the same job for thirty years, driving to it the same way, at least find a new route you
can take once in a while to get there. Do something
to invite newness into your life so you can discover
God's many ways of revealing Himself to you.

Be Led by the Holy Spirit

*For all who are led by the Spirit of God
are sons of God.*

ROMANS 8:14

We live in a society in which people are driven to engage in many activities. We can get almost too tired to move from doing so much in a day, but busyness is not the kind of life to which God has called us.

God will not *drive* us to do things; He will *lead* us by putting in our heart what we are supposed to do. If you follow the Holy Spirit, you may have to say no to some activities that you are saying yes to right now. If what you are doing leaves you drained and worn out, you may not have God's anointing to do it. When He leads you to do something, He will also energize you to fulfill your true call.

Prune your life of things that drain you, and trust God to lead you to the works that keep you growing and healthy.

Change, Don't Complain

All things are legitimate [permissible — and
we are free to do anything we please], but not all
things are helpful (expedient, profitable, and whole-
some). All things are legitimate, but not all things
are constructive [to character] and edifying
[to spiritual life].

1 CORINTHIANS 10:23

People complain about stress, but some people would rather complain than change. It is easy to be frightened at the thought of jumping off life's high-speed treadmill, especially if you aren't sure what to give up in order to slow down your life.

God wants you to enjoy a beautiful life with simplicity, sanity, and clear direction. That only comes by spending time with Him, reading His Word, talking to Him, and listening for His response. If you are too busy to get alone with Him each day, then set some boundaries in your life. Say no to whatever is keeping you from starting your day with God.

Rest Awhile

Come to Me, all you who labor and are heavy-
laden and overburdened, and I will cause you to rest.
[I will ease and relieve and refresh your souls.]

MATTHEW 11:28

Getting stress out of your life takes more than prayer alone. You must take action to make changes and stop doing whatever is causing the stress. You can learn to calm down in the way you handle things.

Jesus invited us to come to Him if we are overburdened. He promised to refresh us if we are weary, worn out, or overworked. Take time to go to Jesus anytime you feel that you are going over the edge of peace and into the pit of stress. Let His presence refill and refresh you.

Come Apart to Stay Together

And the effect of righteousness will be peace
[internal and external], and the result of righ-
teousness will be quietness and confident
trust forever.

ISAIAH 32:17

If you are feeling compelled to do so much that you are physically worn out, you may be driven instead of led. Remember, you have to come apart from a busy routine before you come apart yourself. You have to get away from everything before you come apart physically, mentally, and emotionally. Give yourself time to get a good night's sleep.

It is tempting to do everything that everybody else is doing, be involved in everything, know everything, hear everything, and be everywhere, but it isn't God's best for you. Be willing to separate yourself from compulsive activity before you come apart at the seams! Spend time with God, and ask Him to give order to your day.

Take a Break

*Return to your rest, O my soul, for the Lord
has dealt bountifully with you.*

PSALM 116:7

We all need a break in the action from time to time. Resting isn't just a good idea — it is a command of God: "Six days you shall do your work, but the seventh day you shall rest and keep Sabbath, that your ox and your donkey may rest, and the son of your bondwoman, and the alien, may be refreshed" (Exodus 23:12). The Lord added that "even in plowing time and in harvest you shall rest [on the Sabbath]" (Exodus 34:21)

That means that for one day a week we are to withdraw from common labor and to rest. Don't work that day, even in the busy seasons. Dedicate that day to spending time with God, worshiping Him. Start your week off right by getting back to what is really important — honoring God.

Quality Makes the Difference

*Beloved, let us love one another, for love is
(springs) from God; and he who loves [his fellowmen]
is begotten (born) of God and is coming [progres-
sively] to know and understand God [to perceive
and recognize and get a better and clearer
knowledge of Him].*

1 JOHN 4:7

Sometimes we think that the busier we are, the more we are doing in the kingdom of God. But it is not *how much* we do, it is the *quality* of what we do that makes the difference. Most people will admit that they need to spend more of their time developing good relationships.

You can't be a good friend to somebody if you never put any time into your relationship. Ask God to bring someone to mind that He would like for you to bless today. Then follow through and let that person know that God brought them to your heart.

Rest Is God's Law

Let us therefore be zealous and exert ourselves and
strive diligently to enter that rest [of God, to know
and experience it for ourselves], that no one may fall
or perish by the same kind of unbelief and disobedi-
ence [into which those in the wilderness fell].

HEBREWS 4:11

Don't work so hard that you miss your time with God. Rest is important for your spiritual and physical life. The need for rest can't be ignored; it is a law of God. Just like the laws concerning eating, sowing, and reaping, we cannot break the principle of rest without paying the price of disobedience.

Paul sent Epaphroditus home saying that he came near death through working for Christ (see Philippians 2:25–30), but God had mercy on him and spared his life. Find time to be still on a regular basis. It is in moments of rest that you are most likely to hear God speak to you.

Rest and Renew

So then, there is still awaiting a full and *complete Sabbath-rest reserved for the [true] people of God; for he who has once entered [God's] rest also has ceased from [the weariness and pain] of human labors, just as God rested from those labors peculiarly His own.*

HEBREWS 4:9–10

We all have gifts and talents far beyond what we use, but many of us are so worn out that we don't feel like doing anything. Even God rested from all of His labors, not because He was tired, but just to enjoy His creation (see Genesis 2:1–3). Stop working all the time, and enjoy yourself.

Even the land needs to rest every several years to produce good crops. If you don't rest, you are going to cut down your production and stifle your creativity. You don't have to work at God's plan for you; He will cause it to come to pass (see Philippians 1:6). Rest in Him.

Reenergize Yourself

*Guide me in Your truth and faithfulness and teach
me, for You are the God of my salvation; for You
[You only and altogether] do I wait [expectantly]
all the day long.*

PSALM 25:5

If you are worn out all the time, it will affect your spiritual life because you won't want to pray, study the Word, or walk in the fruit of the Spirit. If you are no longer sensitive to other people's needs, you aren't hearing from God.

If you are this tired, it is time to reenergize your life. Prune away the things that wear you out; don't try to do what you think everyone else is doing. Wait on God to lead you, and get the rest you need to enjoy your walk with Him.

Enjoy Yourself

There is nothing better for a man than that he
should eat and drink and make himself enjoy good
in his labor. Even this, I have seen, is from
the hand of God.

ECCLESIASTES 2:24

We all have things that must be done, but God wants us to enjoy our life's journey. If we are too busy, we will block the flow of what the Holy Spirit wants to do through us.

Busyness keeps us from being fruitful in the kingdom of God. God didn't put us here just to work, strive, accumulate things, and become stressed out. He wants us to enjoy Him and His creation.

Take time to enjoy what God has given you. Enjoy your family, your home, and yourself today.

Move Forward

I do not consider, brethren, that I have captured
and made it my own [yet]; but one thing I do [it is
my one aspiration]: forgetting what lies behind and
straining forward to what lies ahead, I presss on.

PHILIPPIANS 3:13–14

God will anoint you to do what He calls you to do. But when His anointing is gone, let it go. Get rid of the things that God's anointing was on at one time, but not anymore. Don't keep doing the same thing because people expect you to.

I encourage you to prune off activities that fill your day but don't add to your life. Sometimes we hold on to assignments that God is finished with for us. Ask God for wisdom, then walk away from tasks He no longer is asking you to do. Make room for new life to flourish through the work of your hands.

Let God Set Your Agenda

But this thing I did command them: Listen to and obey My voice, and I will be your God and you will be My people; and walk in the whole way that I command you, that it may be well with you.

JEREMIAH 7:23

Remember, you made your schedule, and you can change it. Pray about your day, your week, and your life goals to find out what God wants you to do, and what He doesn't want you to do.

If you don't do what God is telling you to do, you may let people control and manipulate you to do what they want you to do. You may end up doing things for which you are not anointed. If you do what God tells you to do, He will bless you with joy, peace, rest, and wonderful relationships.

Get Rid of Distractions

That which is desired in a man is loyalty and
kindness [and his glory and delight are his giving].

PROVERBS 19:22

Sometimes you may just need to clear
away the clutter so you can clearly see
what is worthwhile. Here is a simple suggestion:
Don't keep more than you can take care of. If you
have so much junk in your home that it takes you
hours to dust it, get rid of something.

Find a big carton and write "Blessing Box" on
the side of it. Start putting extra things into it until
cleaning is more manageable. Find someone who
doesn't have much and bless them. You will be
amazed at how easy it is to start your day right when
you are no longer distracted by things you don't
need.

Get Up and Work

And let the beauty and *delightfulness* and *favor*
of the Lord our God be upon us; confirm and *establish*
the work of our hands — yes, the work of our hands,
confirm and *establish it.*

PSALM 90:17

It is obvious we are supposed to work more than rest. Some people just lie on the couch, eating junk food and watching television all day, and then they wonder why their lives are a wreck.

Once rested, get up and work. You can't take authority over your life if you don't have authority over a sink full of dirty dishes or a messy garage. If you want to grow in ministry to others, the Word says you must get your own house in order first (see 1 Timothy 3:5). Stay home and clean if you need to; but win the battle of getting your life in order before tackling the whole world.

Ministry Is Fulfilling Work

For you shall eat [the fruit] of the labor of your hands; happy (blessed, fortunate, enviable) shall you be, and it shall be well with you.

PSALM 128:2

There is nothing more fulfilling than being rested and ready for the work that God has called us to do. God puts the desire in us to minister to people through whatever work we do. But ministry is work that requires physical, emotional, and spiritual strength.

Hard work is rewarding when you follow God's way and minister to other people through "the labor of your hands." That is why it is so important to start your day with God. His presence will build you up emotionally, His words will strengthen you spiritually, and the time of rest that He calls you to enjoy will make you physically able to handle whatever may come your way.

About the Author

JOYCE MEYER has been teaching the Word of God since 1976 and in full-time ministry since 1980. She is the bestselling author of over 54 inspirational books, including *Secrets to Exceptional Living, The Joy of Believing Prayer,* and *Battlefield of the Mind,* as well as thousands of cassettes and a complete video library. Joyce's *Life In The Word* radio and television programs are broadcast around the world, and she travels extensively conducting "Life In The Word" conferences. Joyce and her husband, Dave, are the parents of four grown children and make their home in St. Louis, Missouri.

To contact the author write:
Joyce Meyer Ministries
P.O. Box 655
Fenton, MO 63026
Or call: (636) 349-0303

Internet Address: www.joycemeyer.org

Please include your testimony of help received
from this book when you write. Your prayer
requests are welcome.

To contact the author in Canada, please write:
Joyce Meyer Ministries Canada, Inc.
Lambeth Box 1300
London, ON N6P 1T5
Or call: (636) 349-0303

In Australia, please write:

Joyce Meyer Ministries-Australia

Locked Bag 77

Mansfield Delivery Centre

Queensland 4122

Or call: 07 3349 1200

In England, please write:

Joyce Meyer Ministries

P.O. Box 1549

Windsor

SL4 1GT

Or call: (0) 1753-831102

Other Joyce Meyer Titles

Jesus — Name Above All Names

"Good Morning, This Is God!" Daily Calendar

Help Me — I'm Married!

Reduce Me to Love

Be Healed in Jesus' Name

How to Succeed At Being Yourself

Eat and Stay Thin

Weary Warriors, Fainting Saints

Life in the Word Journal

Life in the Word Devotional

Be Anxious for Nothing

Be Anxious for Nothing Study Guide

Straight Talk on Loneliness

Straight Talk on Fear

Straight Talk on Insecurity

Straight Talk on Discouragement

Straight Talk on Worry

Straight Talk on Depression

Straight Talk on Stress

Don't Dread

Managing Your Emotions

Healing the Brokenhearted

"Me and My Big Mouth!"

"Me and My Big Mouth!" Study Guide

Prepare to Prosper

Do It Afraid!

Expect a Move of God in Your Life . . . Suddenly!

Enjoying Where You Are on the Way to Where
You Are Going

The Most Important Decision You Will Ever Make

When, God, When?

Why, God, Why?

The Word, the Name, the Blood

Battlefield of the Mind

Battlefield of the Mind Study Guide

Tell Them I Love Them

Peace

The Root of Rejection

Beauty for Ashes

If Not for the Grace of God

If Not for the Grace of God Study Guide